SELF-WORKING
CARD TRICKS

KARL FULVES

SELF-WORKING
CARD TRICKS

72 Foolproof Card Miracles for the
Amateur Magician

WITH 42 ILLUSTRATIONS BY
JOSEPH K. SCHMIDT

DOVER PUBLICATIONS, INC.
NEW YORK

Published in Canada by General Publishing Company, Ltd., 30 Lesmill Road, Don Mills, Toronto, Ontario.
Published in the United Kingdom by Constable and Company, Ltd., 10 Orange Street, London WC 2.

Self-Working Card Tricks is a new work, first published by Dover Publications, Inc., in 1976.

International Standard Book Number: 0-486-23334-0
Library of Congress Catalog Card Number: 75-36371

Manufactured in the United States of America
Dover Publications, Inc.
180 Varick Street
New York, N.Y. 10014

INTRODUCTION

Interest in the art of magic has never been greater than it is today, and because of this many people are being drawn to magic as a hobby. It is with these newcomers in mind that the present collection of card magic was assembled, but whether you are a complete novice or an experienced amateur you will find the material in this book easy to master and enjoyable to perform.

While the subject of the self-working card trick is vast, I have tried to choose tricks that require no skill, not even the rudimentary skill of an overhand shuffle, double lift or any other procedure requiring secret controlled manipulation of the cards. The intent is rather to place before the reader those tricks which he can easily grasp, so that he can begin almost at once to perform for friends and discover how much enjoyment can be had from the performance of magic.

Two points must be emphasized. The first deals with the level of technical knowledge that these tricks call for. In many of the tricks you will note that you are instructed to secretly note a particular card before the trick begins, or to secretly reverse a card in the deck prior to performance of the routine in question. Professional cardmen do not have to set up cards secretly because they have the necessary skill to perform the required secret actions right in front of you.

This is another way of saying that when you gain more knowledge in card magic, you can put that knowledge to use in devising shortcuts while working the tricks in this book. If you decide to go the distance and become an absolute master of card magic, you can do so by acquiring another Dover publication, *Expert Card Technique* by Jean Hugard and Frederick Braue. But if your goal is the entertainment of friends, clients or colleagues, the present collection should be quite satisfactory.

The other point deals with presentation. For most of the tricks, I have sketched in the proper presentation or suggested a presentation idea that can be exploited, but I have not delved into the details of this aspect of the tricks. A Dover book, *Magic and Showmanship* by Henning Nelms, will set the groundwork for those who want to extract maximum entertainment value from the tricks they perform.

No book is created in a vacuum. In this final paragraph I would like to thank the contributors for their generosity in making the tricks available for publication, Joseph K. Schmidt for his expert artwork, and Martin Gardner for his behind-the-scenes work that saw this book become a reality. Finally, I would like to dedicate this book to my magical mentor, J. W. Sarles.

KARL FULVES

CONTENTS

STRANGE SECRETS 79

REVELATIONS 86

MIRACLES WITH CARDS 100

CARD LOCATIONS

In terms of plot, or the effect as seen by the audience, card locations are probably the simplest and most direct card effects. The spectator chooses a card and returns it to the deck. The magician then finds or locates the chosen card. Generally speaking, the manipulator is concerned with two things in the location trick, the means used to secretly determine the identity or position of the chosen card, and the means used to reveal the chosen card to the spectator. In this chapter we will begin with simple card locations and then develop the theme to include more sophisticated mysteries.

1. NO-CLUE DISCOVERY

A spectator chooses a card and returns it to the deck. He then cuts the deck and completes the cut. His card is lost in the pack and no one—not even the magician—knows where the card is.

The magician takes the deck and begins dealing cards one at a time into a face-up heap on the table. As the magician deals, he instructs the spectator to call out the names of the cards. The spectator is asked to give no clue when his selected card shows up. He is not to pause, hesitate, blink or change his facial expression. Nevertheless, the magician claims, he will be able to detect the faintest change in the spectator's tone of voice at the exact instant the chosen card shows up.

The cards are dealt one at a time off the top of the deck. The spectator calls them out as they are dealt. It does not matter how he calls them out; he can disguise his voice, whisper, shout or name the cards in French; when the chosen card turns up, the magician immediately announces that it is the card selected by the spectator.

Method: This trick makes use of a principle known as the Key Card. Before performing the trick, secretly glimpse the bottom card of the deck. This can be done as the deck is being removed from the card case. In Figure 1, the Key Card is the 3D.*

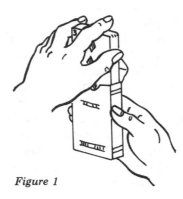

Figure 1

Hold the deck face-down in the left hand. Then spread the cards from left to right, inviting the spectator to choose a card from the center, as in Figure 2.

As the spectator removes his card, separate the deck at the point from which the card was taken; see Figure 3. Tell the spectator to look at his card and remember its identity. As he does this, place the packet of cards in your right hand on the table.

Tell the spectator to replace his card on top of the packet that lies on the table. Your instruction should be something like this: "Please place your card back in its original position in the deck." As you speak, point with the right hand to the tabled packet. As a matter of fact,

---

* The Three of Diamonds. This standard form of reference, with numeral and initial of the suit name, will be used in the book from time to time.

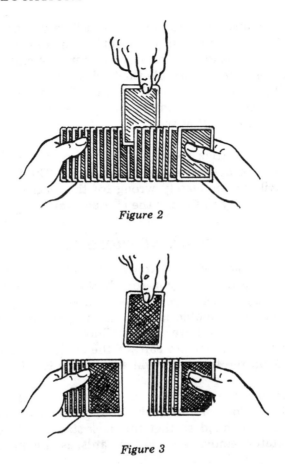

Figure 2

Figure 3

the spectator is *not* returning his card to its original location, but this fact is never questioned.

When the spectator has placed his card on top of the tabled packet, place the packet in your left hand on top of his card. Tell the spectator to carefully square up the deck. His card is apparently lost in the deck, but really it lies directly below the Key Card, the 3D in our example.

Now begin to deal cards off the top of the deck, turning them face-up as you deal. Explain that if the spectator names the cards as they are dealt, you can detect which card is his, no matter how he tries to disguise his

voice. Encourage him to announce each card in a different
manner; he can speak in a dialect or an obscure foreign
tongue; he can shout, scream or whisper. The more variety
he uses, the more impossible the trick seems.

All you need do is wait until the 3D shows up. Then
deal the next card. This will be the spectator's chosen card,
and you announce it as such.

The next trick is a good follow-up routine because
the performer appears to make a mistake. The trick looks
as if it will go completely wrong for the magician, but he
succeeds anyway in finding the chosen card.

2. A SPORTING PROPOSITION

This version of the "No-Clue Discovery" is presented
as a gambling trick. As you shuffle the deck, tell the audience that a gambler once showed you an infallible way to
win a bet. So infallible is this system that the lucky few
who know about it have earned millions of dollars. As you
talk, glimpse the bottom card of the deck and then place
the deck on the table. We will assume the Key Card is the
6C.

Instruct the spectator to remove a packet of cards
from the middle of the deck. Hold the end of the deck
with the right hand so that the deck stays in place while
the spectator removes a packet of cards, as in Figure 4.

Figure 4

Emphasize that you have no way of knowing how
many cards the spectator holds. Then tell him to shuffle
the cards until they are thoroughly mixed. When the spec-

tator is satisfied that the cards are completely mixed, have him note the top card of the packet. He then replaces the packet on top of the deck.

As a further precaution against trickery, tell the spectator to carefully square the deck; then have him cut it and complete the cut. Finally he is to square up the deck once more. The situation appears hopeless, but in fact his chosen card is directly below the Key Card, the 6C in our example.

Again emphasize that your infallible system cannot possibly fail. So sure are you of this system that you would be willing to bet thousands on its success. As you talk, deal cards off the top of the deck. Turn each card face-up as you place it on the table, and overlap the cards so that they are all visible to the spectator, as in Figure 5.

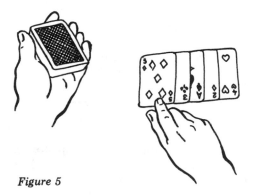

Figure 5

Sooner or later you will turn up the 6C. Do not hesitate or pause in the deal. Place the 6C face-up on the table, deal the next card (the chosen card) and two or three more. Of course, the card you deal right after the 6C is the chosen card, but you do not give any indication that you know this fact. Simply remember the identity of the chosen card as it is turned face-up. For the sake of example, say it is the 2H.

After you have gone several cards past the chosen card, stop dealing, tap the top card of the deck and say, "The next card I turn over will be your card. It's absolutely guaranteed; the system is infallible. I'd offer to bet you a small sum of money on the outcome, but I don't want to take your hard-earned cash. The system never fails."

The spectator will be obviously skeptical of your challenge because he sees his card already on the table. Before he has a chance to say anything, however, you remark, "Remember, I said the next card I turn over will be your card." Reach for the top card of the deck as if you are about to turn it face-up. Then hesitate, withdraw the right hand and immediately drop the hand onto the chosen card. (If you forget the identity of the chosen card, it will be the card immediately to the *right* of the Key Card, from the spectator's point of view; see Figure 6.) Remove the chosen card from the spread and turn *it* over so it is face-down.

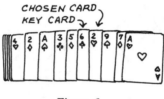

Figure 6

This outcome is completely unexpected by the audience. When you have turned the chosen card over, you can say, "A remarkable system, isn't it?"

3. SPELLO

A different type of location is used here. The identity of the chosen card is not known; instead, position in the deck is controlled by an offbeat means.

Borrow a deck of cards if possible. Then say that you want to be sure there are no jokers in the pack. Turn the pack and spread the cards from left to right. As you pretend to look for jokers, you in fact count the cards, beginning at the face card of the deck, and continue the count until you reach the 12th card from the face.' Note and remember this card, which we'll say is the 8H.

Tell the spectator you would like to write a prediction about the card he is going to select. Pick up a business card and on the blank side write, "This Must Be It." Pick up the deck, fan it and insert the business card directly in back of the card you glimpsed (the 8H in our example); see Figure 7. Do not let the spectator see what you wrote.

Figure 7

Square up the deck and place it face-down on the table. Instruct the spectator to cut off some cards from the top of the deck. Remark that he should cut off less than half.

Tell him to shuffle the cards he cut and to note the top card. Then tell him to drop his packet back on top of the deck and give the deck a cut. When he's done this, take the deck and cut it at the business card, so that the business card becomes the top card. It is easy to cut to the business card; the thickness of the business card forms a natural break or separation in the deck, and you simply cut to this break and complete the cut.

Turn over the business card so the side with the writing is uppermost. Have the spectator read your prediction aloud. You then spell out the prediction message, T – H – I – S – M – U – S – T – B – E – I – T, dealing a card off the top of the deck for each letter in the message. After you have dealt off the card corresponding to the last letter of the message, turn over the next card and it will be the chosen card.

4. THE LAZY MAGICIAN

In this trick the spectator does most of the work. It was a favorite of the stage magician Blackstone, who often presented it by having several spectators invited up on stage to participate. You can do the trick with as many as five spectators, the procedure being the same in each case. For the present, we will assume you are going to present it to just one spectator.

Tell him that sometimes you can spot someone who has the talent to be a magician and that he looks like the type who could be an expert with cards. As you talk, remove ten cards from the top of a freely shuffled deck and hand these to the spectator.

Say that in this trick he is going to do all the hard work. Direct him to shuffle the packet. Then have him look over the cards and decide on one. When he has chosen one, tell him to remember its position from the top of the packet. To take a specific example, assume that when he fans the cards he decides on the 8H. He would then remember that the Eight of Hearts was 6th from the top of the packet, as in Figure 8.

SELECTED
CARD

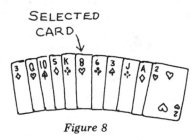

Figure 8

Tell him to square up the packet and hand it to you. When you get it back, say, "We'll give them a cut." Hold the packet face-down in the left hand. Push off the top five cards. Take these as a unit and place them on the bottom of the packet. Then hand the packet back to him.

Have him hold the packet face-down in his left hand. Then tell him to transfer as many cards from top to bottom as the original position of his card. In our example, since his card was 6th from the top of the packet, he would transfer 6 cards, one at a time, from the top to the bottom of the packet.

Now say, "All you have to do is use the elimination shuffle to eliminate every card except the one you picked." The elimination shuffle works like this: he transfers the top card of the packet to the bottom of the packet. Then he takes the next card and places it on the table. He places the next card under the packet and the next onto the table. He continues this elimination shuffle (called an under/down shuffle by magicians because the first card goes under the packet, the next card down on the table, the next card under the packet, etc.) until he has one card remaining in his hand.

Ask him to name the card he chose. He'll say it was the 8H. Have him turn over the card and it is indeed the 8H. Congratulate him on being an outstanding magician.

5. TRAPPED

This is an instance where two magical effects take place, one right after the other, without any moves or sleights. As the audience sees it, the magician openly places the Ace of Spades face-up adjacent to a chosen card, and then cuts the deck. He snaps his fingers and spreads the cards to reveal that the Ace of Spades has changed magically to the Ace of Clubs. The deck is squared up and respread. Now it is seen that *both* of the black Aces are face-up with a face-down card between them. When this card is removed from the deck, it proves to be the chosen card.

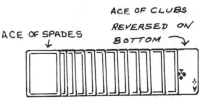

Figure 9

Method: Before doing this trick, secretly bring the Ace of Clubs to the bottom of the deck and reverse it. Place the Ace of Spades on top. Figure 9 shows the condi-

tion of the deck at this point, though you do not of course
reveal the presence of the reversed Ace of Clubs to the
audience.

Remove the top card and place it face-up on the table. Say that the Ace of Spades will aid you in an interest-
ing demonstration of magic. Spread the cards and have the
spectator remove one. Square up the deck and place it
face-down on the table. Then have the spectator place his
card face-down on the table. Place the deck on the top of
his card. You then place the Ace of Spades face-up on top
of the deck.

Give the deck a cut and complete the cut. Then place
the deck in the left hand and spread the cards to the right
until you come to the first reversed Ace. It will be the Ace
of Clubs. Do not spread the cards any further at this point
because you do not want to accidentally expose the Ace of
Spades. When you get to the Ace of Clubs, say, "The Ace
of Spades has changed to the other black Ace."

Square up the deck. Say, "Now let's see if we can get
both of the black Aces to turn face-up." Snap the fingers
and then spread the deck face-down on the table. The two
black Aces will be face-up in the center of the deck with a
face-down card between them. Have the chosen card
named. Then remove the card between the black Aces and
show that the Aces trapped the spectator's card.

6. WHISPERING JOKER

The Joker is inserted face-up into a face-down packet.
The cards on either side of the Joker are remembered by
two spectators. Then the cards are shuffled and the Joker
removed. Placing half the packet in each jacket pocket, the
magician asks the Joker to whisper to him the name of
each chosen card, and also how to find it.

Pretending to hear an instruction from the Joker, the
magician reaches into each jacket pocket and removes the
chosen cards.

Method: This trick, developed by Charles Jordan, exploits a little-known principle in a clever way. You will need a packet of 20 cards plus the Joker. Have the packet shuffled and placed face-down on the table. Ask a spectator to turn the Joker face-up and insert it anywhere in the packet.

Then tell him to pick up the packet, fan the cards so he can see the faces, and remember the card just to the left of the Joker. Have a second spectator remember the card just to the right of the Joker.

When they have done this, take the packet back (the face-up Joker is still in it) and perform the following shuffle. Hold the packet face-down in the left hand and slide the top card to the right. Then slide the next card to the right, but slide it up also so it is upjogged. Slide the third card directly to the right, but upjog the fourth card. Continue in this way, upjogging every other card, until you've gone through the packet. Then separate the upper group of cards from the lower group, placing the upper group on top of the lower group.

Repeat this shuffle exactly as described above. When you have finished, pretend to remember that the reversed or face-up Joker is still in the packet. Remarking that you won't need the Joker, run through the cards until you spot the Joker, then cut the packet at that point so the Joker is on top. Place the Joker face-up on the table.

Have someone cut off about half of the packet from the top and drop it in your left jacket pocket. The other half of the packet is dropped into your right jacket pocket.

Pretend to get "whispered" information from the Joker as to the location and identity of the chosen cards. Actually one of the chosen cards is in the left pocket, exactly five down from the top, while the other chosen card is in the right pocket, exactly five cards up from the bottom. All you need to do is reach into each pocket and remove the proper card.

IMPROMPTU
CARD ROUTINES

Audiences are invariably impressed by the fact that the magician can work with any deck handed to him, without the need for special apparatus or elaborate setting-up procedures. Many of the tricks in this book fit the impromptu category, and some, like "Ultra Coincidence" (No. 27) and "Mental Miracle" (No. 67), can be built up as unfathomable mysteries.

The tricks in this chapter were collected together because they are strictly impromptu and thoroughly tested before audiences for maximum impact. Although they are easy to perform, you will get much more credit for magical powers if you pretend that great skill is involved. At least half of the secret of acquiring a reputation in magic is knowing how to act while presenting the trick.

7. ANY DECK, ANY TIME

Although a trick of honorable ancestry, this card location still rates as one of the most impressive in the entire literature on the subject. In describing it here, I will give a step-by-step procedure that should make it easy for anyone to follow, and at the same time avoid ambiguities that might otherwise mislead the reader.

Any deck is used. Tell a spectator to cut it into three piles. The exact number in each pile is not important, but the piles should be approximately equal in size.

While you turn your back, ask him to pick a pile, shuffle it and note the top card. Then tell him to turn the pile face-up and place it on top of either of the two other piles on the table. When he has done this, have him place the remaining pile face-down on top of all.

The condition of the deck now is that there is a face-up pile of cards sandwiched between two face-down piles. Tell the spectator to carefully square up the deck. Then have him cut off half of the deck and shuffle it into the other half.

Tell him to square the deck after the shuffle and give the deck a cut. At this point the spectator himself can look through the cards and verify that face-up and face-down cards are randomly mixed throughout the deck.

Take the deck from him and turn it over. Run the cards from hand to hand. You will notice that small groups of face-up and face-down cards appear at random in the deck. But you will also note something that the spectator will never spot; there is a long run of face-up cards in the deck, longer than any other run.

As you study the cards, pretending to look for his card, cut the deck so all of this long run of face-up cards has been brought to the face of the deck nearest you. Now beginning at the face of the deck, run the cards from left to right until you come to the last face-up card in this long run. The next card (a face-down card) will be the spectator's card. Reveal it as dramatically as you can.

8. MENTAL MATES

Two shuffled decks are used. One is red-backed, the other blue-backed. Both may be borrowed and both are shuffled by the spectator. The two red Aces are removed from the red-backed deck, turned face-up, and inserted back into the deck so they are on either side of a face-down card. No one knows the identity of this face-down card between the red Aces.

The magician now removes the two red Aces from the blue deck and places them on either side of a face-down

card from that deck. Both decks are handed to the spectator. He removes the card between the red Aces in one deck
and finds this card to be the Ten of Spades. Then he
removes the random card between the red Aces in the
other deck and finds that it too is the Ten of Spades.

What makes this trick so impressive is the fact that it
is performed under the most stringent test conditions, using borrowed, shuffled cards.

Method: Borrow two decks and have them well
mixed by the spectator. Ask him to remove the red Aces
from the red deck. Then have him shuffle the deck once
more, just to be certain he has not accidentally seen any
cards. Now tell him to spread the deck face-down and
place the red Aces face-up on either side of a card, as
shown in Figure 10.

Figure 10

Note in Figure 10 that the red Aces are upjogged
about one inch. Tell the spectator to leave them in that
condition. Then square up the deck, still leaving the Aces
upjogged.

Hold the deck face-up in the left hand. Remind the
spectator that he placed the two red Aces on either side of
a completely unknown card in the pack. Hold the back of
the deck to him so he can see the face of the red Aces.
Then with the right hand slowly push the Aces into the
pack. Referring to Figure 11, you will find that as the red
Aces are being pushed flush with the deck, the card between them will slide out of the deck just far enough for
you to glimpse its identity. In Figure 11, this card is the
Ten of Spades. This subtle method of glimpsing the spectator's card is the ingenious invention of Martin Gardner.

Once you have spotted the spectator's card, square up
the deck and turn it face-up. Pick up the blue-backed deck

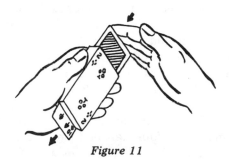

Figure 11

and turn it face-up. Find the two red Aces, but as you do, spot the Ten of Spades in this deck and note how far away it is from one of the Aces. For example, it may be seven cards below the Ace of Hearts.

Upjog the red Aces. Then square up the deck and turn it face-down. Spread it face-down again and say that you will place the red Aces at a random position in this deck. Remove the Ace of Diamonds and turn it face-up. You know that the duplicate Ten of Spades is seven cards down from the Ace of Hearts, so count seven cards and place the face-up Ace of Diamonds on one side of the Ten of Spades. Then remove the upjogged Ace of Hearts, turn it face-up and place it on the other side of the Ten of Spades. Of course, the Ten of Spades is face-down, so the audience assumes you are placing the red Aces on either side of a completely unknown card.

Hand both decks to the spectator. Have him remove the card between the red Aces in each pack. Then have each of these cards turned face-up to reveal they are the Ten of Spades.

9. DEUCES WILD

The four deuces are removed from any deck. A spectator initials the face of each deuce to guard against the magician's switching cards. The spectator then shuffles the deuces so the packet is thoroughly mixed.

He chooses a deuce from the packet, returns it to the packet, and further shuffles the packet. The deuces are then handed to the magician. Without fail, the magician names the deuce chosen by the spectator.

The trick is repeated immediately, and once again the magician correctly identifies the deuce chosen by the spectator.

Method: Proceed as written above by having the spectator remove the four deuces from the deck. Ask him to write his initials across the middle of each deuce. Then he is to gather the deuces one on top of the next, turn them face-down and mix them.

Take them from him. Spread them face-down between the hands and have him choose one. While he looks at it, square up the remainder of the packet. The secret comes into play at this point. Simply turn the packet around end for end. All attention is on the spectator at this point, so your action of turning the packet around is not noticed.

Have the chosen deuce returned to the packet. Then hand the packet to the spectator and have him mix the cards. When he's done this, take back the packet and hold it so that you alone can see the faces of the cards. On three of the deuces the spectator's initials will be right-side-up. On the fourth deuce the initials will be upside down. This will be the chosen deuce. Of course, the reason why the initials run one way on three of the cards and the opposite way on the chosen card is that you turned the packet around end for end after the chosen card was removed from the packet.

Once you know the identity of the chosen deuce, reveal it as impressively as possible. Do *not* remove the chosen deuce from the packet or otherwise tamper with the packet. Assuming that the chosen deuce was the Two of Hearts, for example, name this deuce as the chosen one, turn the packet face-down and immediately offer to repeat the trick.

Again spread the cards and have a deuce selected. As

it is being shown to the audience, square up the packet and turn it end for end. Have the chosen deuce returned to the packet. Then invite the spectator to mix up the cards.

When he is satisfied that they are well mixed, take back the packet and fan it so you alone can see the faces. Look for the Two of Hearts. The initials will point right side up or upside down. It does not matter which, but make sure you know which way the initials point. Then simply look for the other deuce in the packet that has the initials pointing the same way. There will be only one other such deuce and it will be the deuce chosen the second time.

There is one exception. If the Two of Hearts points the same way as the other three deuces, you know that the second time the spectator again chose the Two of Hearts. When you reveal the card the second time, make the most of this astounding coincidence.

10. RAPID TRANSIT

Transpositions are those tricks where two or more cards change places. Generally a good deal of skill is required, but the following trick, devised by J. W. Sarles and the author, accomplishes the transposition without skill.

Have a borrowed deck shuffled. While it is being shuffled, secretly note the bottom card. We will say this card is the King of Hearts. Assuming the spectator is sitting across the table from you, ask him to remove his favorite Ace and place it on top of the deck. His favorite Ace may be the Ace of Spades. When he's placed it on top of the pack, ask him to note and remember the bottom card of the deck also. After he's done this, tell him to hand you the deck under the table.

Grasp the deck from above by the near ends, more or less as shown in Figure 4. Tell the spectator to remember the identity of his favorite Ace. As you talk, secretly turn the right hand over so it is palm-up. This also reverses the deck.

Tell the spectator to remove his favorite Ace from the top of the deck. He reaches under the table and removes what he thinks is the top card. But since you turned the deck over, he has removed the bottom card (in our example, the King of Hearts).

Once he's removed the card, you turn the right hand palm-down again. Tell him to insert the Ace into the center of the deck. When he has pushed the card into the center, secretly turn the deck over again so it is face-up under the table.

Now tell him to remove the bottom card and hold it in his hand. He removes what he thinks is the bottom card. Take the deck and place it face-down on the table. Then reach under the table and take the card from the spectator, remarking, "I want to see what card I'm going to work with to find your favorite Ace."

When you take the card from him, pretend to look at it. Say, "All right, the King of Hearts." Here you name the card you secretly glimpsed on the bottom of the deck at the beginning of the trick. Place the card back under the table. The right hand then raps against the tabletop from below. It then comes up into view, holding the card face-down. Turn it over to show it has changed into the spectator's favorite Ace.

For the finish, have him spread the deck face-down on the table. He should be surprised to discover that the King of Hearts is now reversed in the center of the deck.

You may wonder why, at the beginning of the trick, the spectator was asked to place his favorite Ace on top, since the trick would obviously work just as well with any two cards. The reason is that since he is being asked to remember two cards, you want to make it as easy as possible for him. Thus you ask him to place his favorite Ace or his lucky Ace on top of the deck. Since this card is easily remembered, the spectator will find it no trouble to also remember the bottom card of the deck.

You can also have him initial each card with a pencil at the beginning of the routine. To the average layman, initialed cards eliminate such trickery as duplicate cards. But of course it makes no difference in this trick whether the cards are initialed or not.

11. Z-RAY

Using any shuffled deck, the magician writes a mystic symbol on the face of a card. A spectator then initials the face of this card. While the magician turns his back, the spectator places the mystic card anywhere in the deck. The magician then turns around. He explains that the mystic symbol confers an eyeless vision known as z-rays to the person who drew the symbol.

To demonstrate that this is so, the magician slowly deals cards off the top of the deck. At some point he stops. When the next card is turned up, it proves to be the card bearing the mystic symbol. Remember that this is done with any borrowed, shuffled deck handed to you, and there is positively no preparation. The cards are borrowed and the trick immediately commences exactly as written. Further, it may be repeated instantly.

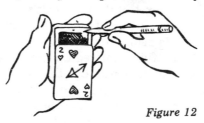

Figure 12

Method: Take the borrowed, shuffled deck and hold it face-down in your left hand. Follow the handling carefully because it is designed to direct audience attention away from the secret. Explain that mystic symbols sometimes have a power of their own which they can convey to those skilled in the art of magic. To illustrate, turn the top card of the deck face-up and place it on top of the deck.

The card may be the Two of Hearts. Note in Figure 12 that the Two of Hearts is not placed squarely on top of

the deck but is backjogged slightly. Borrow a pencil. Say
that you will inscribe the symbol for eyeless vision on the
face of the card. Inscribe a mystic-seeming symbol like the
one shown in Figure 12. But as soon as you finish drawing
the symbol, place a tiny dot on the white border of the
next card, exactly as shown in Figure 12. This method of
secretly marking a card is credited to Glen Gravatt.

The throw-off comes in at this point. The tiny dot is
visible to no one but yourself, so do not be afraid that
anyone will spot it. Hand the pencil to the spectator and
tell him to place his initials on the face of the Two of
Hearts, as this sometimes strengthens the spell. Do *not*
adjust the Two of Hearts or try to hide the secret pencil-
dot. This draws attention to the cards and is exactly what
you want to avoid.

After the spectator has initialed the Two of Hearts,
turn this card face-down on top of the deck. Place the
deck face-down on the table. Ask the spectator to deal
cards off the top into a heap on the table. He deals a card
at a time, beginning with the top card (the Two of Hearts)
and continues the deal for as long as he likes. When he
stops dealing, tell him to take the dealt packet and place it
back on top of the deck. The card bearing the mystic
symbol is thus buried somewhere in the deck.

When he's carefully squared up the deck, take it from
him and begin dealing cards off the top one at a time.
Sooner or later you will spot the card bearing your pencil
dot. Deal this card onto the tabled heap. Then pause dramatically and turn up the next card. It will be the Two of
Hearts.

If you wish to repeat this routine, pick up the tabled
packet and replace it on top of the deck. Then place the
Two of Hearts face-down on top of the deck. The trick can
now be repeated exactly as described above.

12. MATCHING MATCHES

This trick and the next one illustrate how the same effect can be brought about in different ways. This version is based on an ingenious idea of Jack Avis.

Besides the deck of cards, you will need a packet of matches that contains 13 matches, and another that contains eight matches. The number in each packet is not important just as long as the number of matches in both packets *total* 21.

Tear out the matches from both packets and combine them in a heap on the table. Have someone shuffle and cut a deck of cards. Then, while your back is turned, have this spectator remove any number of matches from the group, count them and place them out of sight in his pocket. Invite a second spectator to count the remaining matches, and then conceal them in his pocket. Thus the first spectator may have 14 matches and the second spectator seven matches.

Explain to spectator "A" that you are going to deal cards, one at a time, off the top of the deck. He is to remember the card that falls in a position corresponding to the number of matches he holds. In our example he would remember the 14th card you deal.

Deal cards one at a time off the top of the deck into a face-up heap on the table. Continue the deal until you have dealt at least 18 cards. Ask spectator "A" if he remembers his card. Then square up the face-up heap, turn it over and replace it on top of the deck.

Now ask spectator "B" to remember a card corresponding to the number of matches he holds. In the above example he would remember the 7th card you deal. As before, deal off the top of the deck a card at a time, dealing the cards one on top of each other in a face-up heap. After you've dealt 18 cards pick up the face-up heap, turn it face-down and replace it on top of the deck.

Explain to the audience that although you don't know either card, you will attempt to adjust the positions of both cards without looking at them and without know-ing which card each spectator is thinking of. Place the deck under the table or behind the back. Pretend to adjust cer-tain cards but in fact do nothing.

Bring the deck into view and deal the top ten cards into a heap on the table. Place the balance of the deck alongside the ten-card packet. Explain that you are going to deal cards off the top of both packets. When either spectator sees his card, he is to call stop. If you are lucky, both cards will turn up at exactly the same instant.

All that remains is to deal cards off the top of each packet. If you handled the trick exactly as described, the thought-of cards will turn up simultaneously.

13. THE MAGIC 13

This trick is the creation of Sam Schwartz. It pro-duces the same type of effect as in the above routine, but takes a different path to achieve the end result.

Explain that the number 13 possesses properties both lucky and unlucky, both common and mysterious. To il-lustrate one of the mysterious properties, have someone deal 13 cards from the top of any shuffled deck. While you turn your back, have this fellow remove a portion of the 13-card packet and hand the balance of the packet to an-other spectator.

Each spectator counts the cards he holds and remem-bers the number. Let's say that spectator "A" remembers that he has 5 cards, and spectator "B" remembers that he has 8 cards. Of course the magician is unaware of how many cards each person holds.

Ask that "A's" cards be placed face-down on the ta-ble. Then have "B's" cards placed face-down on top of "A's" cards. Request either spectator to give the 13-card packet a good shuffle just to make sure the cards are well mixed. Then take the packet and deal the cards one at a time off the top into a face-up heap. Ask "A" and "B" to remember the card at the position corresponding to the number each person has in mind. In this case, "A" would remember the 5th card you deal and "B" would remember the 8th card you deal.

When you've dealt all 13 cards into a face-up heap, turn the heap face-down and then deal the packet into two face-down heaps, alternating a card to each heap, dealing first to the left, then to the right, then to the left, then to the right, etc. When you finish dealing the 13 cards, you will have a heap of seven cards on the left, a heap of six cards on the right.

Turn the left-hand heap (the one with seven cards) face-up. Simultaneously deal cards off the top of each heap. When one spectator sees his card being dealt off the face-up heap, he is to call stop. When he does, show that the corresponding card you've just dealt off the face-down heap is the other spectator's chosen card.

POKER DEALS

The lure of gambling is universal. You will even find that when you have done a few card tricks for friends that at least one person is certain to remark that he would not want to play cards with you.

This chapter treats a number of poker deals, two methods of revealing the Aces, a demonstration of cheating at Bridge, and closes with a trick that packs a double punch; not only does the magician instantly change a Straight to a Royal Flush, he shows in a surprising way how the switch was accomplished.

As a rule the more technical gambling tricks appeal only to people who gamble. For that reason, and because many people are not fully acquainted with the more intricate aspects of gambling and odds, the tricks in this chapter were selected because they do not demand special knowledge of gambling. The routines are easy to follow and seem to demonstrate dazzling skill with the pasteboards.

Not included in this chapter are tricks using dice as well as cards. But you will find such tricks elsewhere in the book—"Fate #1" (No. 40), "Fate #2" (No. 41), "Blind Dice #1" (No. 43) and "Blind Dice #2" (No. 44)—and with very little effort you can work them into gambling demonstrations to show how thieves and hustlers exert mental control over dice as well as cards.

14. LESSON IN LARCENY

This trick of Roy Walton's and the next routine, "Automatic Poker," illustrate how radically different methods can be exploited to bring about similar effects. In this case the spectator is given a packet of cards and is told to deal five of them to himself. He can take any five, and when he does he will be surprised to discover that he's dealt himself a Straight!

Preparation is simple. Before starting the trick, arrange to have the 9H – 8S – 7D – 6C & 5D on top of the deck in that order from the top down. Thus, the top card of the deck will be the 9H. Place the deck in its case until ready to perform.

Offer to teach the spectator to become a card sharper in just a few minutes. Remove the deck from its case and openly run through the cards, taking out the 5H – 6S – 7H – 8C – 9D. Arrange them in numerical order with the five as the top card of the packet and the 9D as the bottom card.

Fan the five cards and show them to the spectator. Then square them up and drop the packet onto the table. Remark that you will use five more cards, and as you say this, deal the top five cards of the deck onto the packet that lies on the table.

The balance of the deck is placed aside. Hand the spectator the ten-card packet. Tell him to cut it and complete the cut. Have him do this several times so no one could possibly know the order of any cards in the packet. Then tell him that a good card sharper can of course deal off the top or the bottom as the occasion demands. Naturally the spectator cannot be expected to perform a perfect bottom deal, but you will allow him the option of taking either the top or the bottom card.

Tell the spectator to take five cards for himself. Emphasize that he can take some cards from the top and some from the bottom, or he can take all five cards from the top, or all five from the bottom, or he may decide not to bottom deal at all. In this last case, if he decides to deal honestly, he would simply deal out two poker hands in the conventional fashion.

Regardless of which way he decides to deal, he will always get a Straight. While he looks at his cards, drop your hand on top of the deck and comment, "I wouldn't want to play cards with you."

15. AUTOMATIC POKER

In recent times the demonstration of dealing the winning hand at poker has developed in an unexpected direction; nowadays the magician can allow the spectator the opportunity to pick cards completely at random, and still guarantee that he will get a pat hand. Not only that, the magician can even predict ahead of time exactly which kind of poker hand the spectator will get. Finally the spectator deals the magician an even better hand!

As the audience sees it, the magician writes a prediction and drops it into a glass so it is on view at all times. He then allows the spectator a completely random choice of cards from a packet of different cards. The spectator can take any five cards he desires—there is absolutely no restriction on his choice of cards. He might end up with a King-high Straight. The prediction is opened and it is found that the magician predicted the spectator would choose exactly that, a King-high Straight. Then the magician shows his own hand and it is an Ace-high Straight!

A simple set-up does all the work. Beforehand, stack the top 11 cards as follows from the top down: KD – 10S – 10H – JC – JD – QS – QC – 9H – 9C – AH – KH. Place this packet face-down on top of the face-down deck. The top card of the assembled deck is the KD.

Tell the spectator you'd like to show him something you learned from a gambler. Push over the top cards of the deck, silently counting them until you have pushed over 11 cards. Take these 11 cards into the right hand. The left hand then places the rest of the deck on the table, and the packet of 11 cards is returned to the left hand. Do not call attention to the number of cards in the packet.

Explain that you will use five pairs of cards, all different. With the left thumb push the top two cards over to the right. These two cards are taken by the right hand and shown to the spectator. The pair will consist of a King and a Ten. Do not reverse the order of the cards when you take them into the right hand. Simply take them, show them to the spectator and replace them on the bottom of the packet. If done correctly, the bottom card of the packet will now be the 10S.

Repeat with each of the next four pairs of cards. As you do, point out that each pair contains different cards. Tell the spectator that he is going to have the opportunity to pick his own hand. But to illustrate the power of subliminal suggestion, you claim that you can determine ahead of time exactly which kind of hand he will get—in other words, two pair, a Flush, one pair, or any other combination.

On a slip of paper write, "You will deal yourself a King-high Straight." Fold the paper in half and in half again and drop it in a glass so it is on display and obviously isolated from any tampering that magicians are always accused of using.

Now take the top pair of cards in the right hand. Ask the spectator to choose one card of the pair. Both cards are of course face-down and you do not allow the spectator to see the faces of the cards. He picks a card and places it face-down before him. You then take the remaining card of the pair and place it under the packet.

Repeat this procedure with the next four pairs of cards. Each time the spectator gets a free choice of which card in the pair he wants, and each time you place the remaining card under the packet.

When the spectator has five cards, drop the remainder of the packet on top of the deck. Let the spectator turn his hand over and arrange it to show that he has a King-high Straight. Let him open the prediction and verify that you predicted exactly which hand he would get.

Then say, "You made only one mistake. The five cards you left me with make an even better hand." Deal the top five cards off the deck and turn them over to show that you beat him with an Ace-high Straight.

16. NAMING THE ACES

The spectator shuffles the deck. Then the magician says he can guess the suit of the first Ace that the spectator will deal. The magician names the Ace of Hearts. The spectator deals cards off the top of the deck until he comes to the first Ace. It is the Ace of Hearts.

The Ace of Hearts is placed aside. The spectator assembles the deck and gives it another shuffle. Challenging the odds, the magician offers to repeat the trick and correctly guess the suit of the first Ace that will turn up on this round, saying it will be the Ace of Spades. The spectator deals the cards one at a time off the top. When he turns up the first Ace, it is indeed the Ace of Spades.

"There are two Aces left in the deck," the magician says. "I'll bet you turn up the Ace of Clubs before you get to the Ace of Diamonds." The spectator deals cards one at a time off the top of the deck, and sure enough the Ace of Clubs turns up before the Ace of Diamonds.

Note that the entire trick takes place with the cards in the spectator's hands, and further that he shuffles the deck repeatedly, making it a challenging feat and one that will be of special interest to any spectator interested in seeing the laws of chance overcome.

Method: Arrange the four Aces on top of the deck in Hearts, Spades, Clubs, Diamonds order. Then remove any three cards from the center of the deck and place these on top of the Aces. This is the only preparation.

Hand the deck to someone who plays cards and can be counted on to give the deck a good, even riffle shuffle. Generally he will be a card player or someone interested in gambling, so he will find this demonstration of particular interest.

Tell him that you've made a study of the laws of probability and think you can outwit the odds. Have the spectator give the deck a riffle shuffle. Then say that you will ask him to turn cards face-up one at a time off the top of the deck and that the first Ace he turns up (here you pretend to make a mental calculation) will be the Ace of Hearts.

The spectator deals cards onto the table until he gets to the first Ace. It will be the Ace of Hearts. Have him place this card aside. Then tell him to pick up the dealt cards and replace them face-down on top of the deck. Thus far the demonstration has proven nothing; you could have an infallible system as you claim, or you could be merely lucky.

Instruct the spectator to cut off the top half of the deck and riffle shuffle it into the bottom half. This is quite impressive because after the second shuffle the audience thinks the deck is really well mixed.

Remark that according to your system, the first Ace he will turn up this time should be the Ace of Spades. The spectator deals cards one at a time off the top of the deck. The first Ace he comes to will indeed be the Ace of Spades.

Right at this point say, "There are two Aces left in the deck. It's even money, but I'm so sure of my system, I'll bet a million to one that of the remaining two Aces in the deck, you'll turn up the Ace of Clubs first."

Let the spectator continue dealing until he comes to an Ace. It will be the Ace of Clubs.

17. THE THREE-JACKS DEAL

This routine resulted from collaboration between Lin Searles, the brilliant West Coast magician, and the author. Although based on an old theme, the handling has been streamlined and a logical finish added to the basic routine.

The effect is that you deal two hands of cards, one hand to yourself and one to the spectator. Each hand consists of three cards. On the first round the spectator gets a

10-high Straight. The hands are dropped on top of the deck and you immediately deal two hands again. This time the spectator gets a Straight but it has improved and is now a Jack-high Straight.

The deal is repeated several times and each time, although there is no shuffling, cutting or "stacking" of the deck, the spectator's hand keeps getting better and better. On the final deal he gets an Ace-high Straight, the highest possible Straight. You remark that you hate to lose, and turn over your hand to reveal three Jacks.

Method: A simple set-up and a bit of handling does all the work. The nine-card stack, from the top of the deck down, is as follows: 9 – K – 8 – J – 10 – Q – J – A – J. The set-up is relatively easy to obtain since suits are not important in this routine. The handling is as follows:

1. Patter about the fact that what is called beginner's luck is no myth but a scientific fact. Ask someone who has never played cards to sit opposite you at the table. Explain that you will demonstrate how beginner's luck operates in a real card game.

2. Deal two hands of three cards each, dealing in the conventional manner, alternating a card between the player and yourself. When each player has three cards, place the deck down.

3. Turn up the beginner's hand and show that it contains a Straight consisting of an Eight, Nine and Ten. Remark that a Straight is an excellent hand in any game of Poker. The fact that the spectator got the Straight the very first deal is merely proof that beginner's luck is working for him.

4. Place the beginner's hand face-down on top of yours and place the combined packet on top of the deck.

5. Now repeat Steps 2 and 3 above. Turn up the beginner's hand and show that he has a better Straight, consisting of the Nine, Ten and Jack.

6. Repeat Step 4 in gathering the hands and returning them to the top of the deck.

7. Deal out a new round and show that the begin-

ner's Straight has improved again, consisting now of a Ten, Jack and Queen.

8. Gather the hands as described in Step 4 and deal out two hands again. Now the beginner has a Straight consisting of the Jack, Queen and King. It is here, while all attention is on the spectator's hand, that the secret maneuver is performed. As you point to the spectator's poker hand, simply drop the deck on the dealer's hand. Pay no attention to this secret maneuver. Continue to call attention to the remarkable luck experienced by the beginner.

9. Pick up the beginner's hand, turn it face-down and drop it on top of the deck. Immediately deal out two hands again. Before you turn up the beginner's hand, ask him if he has a hunch as to what his hand will consist of this time. Since his hand has been improving right along, he will make the logical guess, saying that this time he expects an Ace-high Straight.

10. Turn his hand face-up and show that he does indeed have an Ace-high Straight, the highest Straight he can be dealt, consisting of the Queen, King and Ace.

11. Then remark that you hate to lose. Turn up your hand and show that you have dealt yourself three of a kind, specifically, three Jacks.

Note that even if someone should suspect the possibility of your switching cards in Step 8, there is a throw-off in Step 10 because two of the three cards dealt to the spectator in the previous hand will show up in the hand again in Step 10. This would seem to rule out the possibility of any kind of switch, thus making the appearance of the three Jacks in your hand that much more surprising.

18. CUTTING THE ACES

Many of the more spectacular methods of cutting to the Aces require a degree of skill and knowledge that is outside the range of the present book, but the following trick achieves a similar end without the need for great manipulative ability. The trick embodies a double climax in that the spectator succeeds in locating the four Kings, with the magician then locating the four Aces.

Arrange beforehand to have the four Kings on the bottom of the deck with the four Aces in back of them. Ask the spectator to cut the deck into four approximately equal packets. The arrangement will look like Figure 13,

Figure 13

and we will assume the stack of Kings and Aces lies at the bottom of packet "D." In other words, "D" is the original bottom quarter of the deck.

Instruct the spectator to pick up the packet at "A" and to deal a card off the top to position "A," then a card to position "B," then a card to position "C," and then a card to position "D." He continues dealing to all four positions in turn until he has used up all the cards in the packet.

Now he picks up the cards at position "B" and repeats the same dealing procedure. When he's done this, have him pick up the packet at "C" and go through identically the same dealing procedure. He then repeats the procedure with the packet at "D."

At the finish you will again have four heaps of cards on the table. Turn up the top card of each heap. The spectator will be surprised to discover that these cards are the four Kings.

Say, "You did quite well in locating the Kings. Even more remarkable, you left me with the Aces." After giving the spectator the four Kings, turn up the top card of each packet. This time reveal the four Aces for a strong finish.

19. THE BRIDGE HUSTLER

Card experts can exert almost total control over a deck of cards during the process of shuffling and cutting the deck in preparation for a game of bridge. Insiders who hustle bridge tournaments know so many ways of cheating at the game that it is virtually impossible to devise sufficient safeguards against their methods. The following is a simplified method of demonstrating how bridge cheats ply their trade.

It is necessary first to set up the deck. The deck will later be shuffled, so it will appear that all possibility of a set-up is impossible. The set-up is accomplished like this: first remove all of the Clubs from the deck and place them aside. Then stack the remaining cards in the order Hearts-Spades-Diamonds-Hearts-Spades-Diamonds, and so on, the basic Hearts-Spades-Diamonds cycle repeated throughout the deck.

When you have stacked the Hearts, Spades and Diamonds as outlined above, drop the clubs on top of the deck. Place the deck in its case and you are ready to begin.

To set the stage, it is necessary to get the conversation around to the game of bridge, and how, at every tournament, there is talk of cheating. Offer to explain how the bridge hustler works. As you talk, remove the deck from the case.

Fan the cards so you can see the faces. Push off the top thirteen cards (the Clubs) and take them with one hand. Riffle shuffle them into the balance of the deck and square up the pack. Hand the deck to anyone for a fair cut. Say, "First they give the deck a good shuffle and a cut. But unknown to those present, the hustler has one suit marked. Let's say it's Clubs."

Run through the deck and toss out the Clubs as you come to them. Place the Club packet on the table in front of you. "Therefore," you continue, "he knows when a Club is coming up and he can second deal or bottom deal to make sure he gets a pat hand."

Pass the remainder of the deck to a spectator for a final cut. Then tell him to deal the deck into three hands to represent the other three hands in a bridge game.

"But the bridge expert doesn't need to hustle. By means of the shuffles and cuts I illustrated just now, although they look fair, the bridge expert has complete control over the cards. He doesn't even have to deal."

By this time the spectator will have dealt out the three bridge hands. Turn over each to show a truly amazing result; one hand contains all Hearts, the next all Spades, and the last all Diamonds.

20. ACES UP

At the conclusion of some previous trick using the four Aces, drop the Aces on top of the deck, and then relate a story of how a gambler got challenged when he tried to cheat in a game.

First, you explain, he had to stack the Aces. When you say this, deal the top four cards into a face-down row on the table. Then deal a card onto each Ace and then deal another card onto each Ace. At this point you have four heaps of cards on the table, and each heap contains three cards with an Ace on the bottom of each heap.

Gather the four heaps together by placing the heap at the far left on top of the next heap, then this combined heap onto the next, and finally this combined heap onto the last heap.

"While the gambler was stacking the cards, one of the other players became suspicious and took the cards. Just to see if the gambler stacked the Aces, this fellow decided to deal out four hands." Deal four hands of cards, dealing from left to right, until you've again dealt four heaps of three cards each.

"When the suspicious player looked at the hands, he was satisfied that the gambler didn't stack the Aces." Turn each hand up and show that each contains only one Ace.

Then turn each hand face-down in place. Gather the hands from left to right, exactly as described above.

"The gambler asked what the suspicious player hoped to find. The player said he thought the Aces were being stacked." Deal out four hands again. When you've done this, pick up the *last* hand you dealt, the one at the far right, and turn it face-up. Show the three cards and say, "The gambler remarked that he wasn't stacking the Aces to fall into his hand."

Replace the three cards face-down in their original position on the table. Then gather the hands from left to right just as you did before. "The gambler didn't have to stack the Aces because he was keeping them on top where he could switch them in when he needed them." Deal the top four cards face-up onto the table to reveal the four Aces.

21. POKER EXPERT OUTDONE

The creation of Sam Schwartz, this trick is so constructed that it appears as if you are possessed of the uncanny ability to instantly change a mediocre poker hand into a Royal Flush. But the trick is self-working, and even better, contains an unexpected kicker that elevates it to the miracle class.

We will assume you are using a red-backed deck. Remove the Ace of Hearts, King of Spades, Queen of Spades, Jack of Spades and Ten of Spades. Arrange these five cards in Ace-King-Queen-Jack-Ten order from top to bottom. Then remove the Ace of Spades from a blue-backed deck and place it face-down on top of the face-down packet. This complete packet of six cards is placed in your jacket pocket along with the cased red-backed deck until you are ready to perform.

To properly present the trick, first remove the red-backed deck from the pocket and perform a few tricks. Then remark that you would like to relate a story to the audience involving a friend of yours who played poker. In polite circles he would be called a good card handler, but the truth was that he cheated. For example, you say, one night he dealt himself this hand.

Now reach into your pocket, remove the six-card packet and hold it face-up in the left hand. Be careful not to flash the back of the packet. Say, "Using underhanded methods of cheating, he dealt himself a rather good hand, Ace-high Straight." Remove the Ten from the face of the packet with the right hand and turn it over. Say, "Naturally he used marked cards, as you can clearly see. That's how he got this black Ten . . . ."

Keeping the Ten face-up, transfer it to the back of the packet. This brings the Jack of Spades into view. You continue by saying, ". . . and this black Jack . . . ." Take the face-up Jack with the right hand and transfer it to the back of the packet.

". . . A black Queen . . . ." Transfer the Queen to the back of the packet, keeping it face-up as you did with the other cards. ". . . A black King . . . ." Transfer the black King from the face to the back of the packet.

". . . And a red Ace." Stop right here so the audience sees the Ace of Hearts on the face of the packet. Then turn the packet over end for end and place it face-down in the left hand. Say, "He wasn't satisfied with a mere Ace-high Straight." Take the Ace of Hearts off the bottom of the packet, turn it face-up and place it face-up on top of the face-down packet. The position of the cards in the left hand is shown in Figure 14. The left hand is palm-up, fingers together as indicated.

"So by using palming, switches and other methods too unethical to discuss in front of a nice audience like this, he switched the Straight for an unbeatable poker hand."

As you say this, the left hand is swiftly turned palm-down and it slaps its cards onto the top of the face-down deck, as in Figure 15.

Take the left hand away. An Ace of Spades will show face-up. To the average spectator it will look as if you used

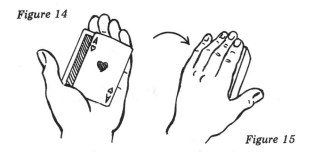

Figure 14

Figure 15

amazing skill to switch out the Ace of Hearts. Without
hesitation deal the Ace of Spades off the top of the deck,
then the Ten, Jack, Queen and King of Spades to display
the Royal Flush in Spades. The transformation of the
Straight to a Royal Flush is so dramatic that it will invariably get a round of applause from the audience.

Acknowledge the applause, then reveal the kicker.
"But my friend went too far. In his haste to switch cards,
he made a fatal mistake." Turn the Ten, Jack, Queen and
King of Spades face-down to show that they have red
backs. This is as it should be, of course. "When he
switched in the Ace, he switched it from the wrong deck."
Slowly turn the Ace of Spades face-down to show that it
has a blue back. You are almost assured of a sensational
round of applause at this point. For the tag line you can
say, "Funny thing, he doesn't play poker much any
more."

COINCIDENCE TRICKS

The coincidence trick is one where the magician and a spectator each happen to choose the same card. In a variation of the basic premise, the trick can end with two different cards found in the same position in two different decks. Both aspects of this basic theme will be discussed in this chapter. It should be emphasized that the coincidence effect is one of the strongest in card magic. Since such tricks involve the simultaneous revelation of *two* cards rather than one, any thought of manipulation or control on the magician's part appears to be completely out of the question.

22. DO AS I DO

Under the heading of the "Do as I Do" trick is a type of card effect using two decks of contrasting back design or color. If you own a set of bridge cards, you will find that the backs of the decks are different colors. For this trick we will assume that one deck is red-backed and the other deck blue-backed. Since such contrasting decks are usually available when people get together to play bridge, this type of card effect is particularly suitable after an evening of bridge.

The following routine is the basic or classic form of the two-deck card trick, in which it turns out that the magician and the spectator choose the same card under seemingly impossible conditions.

The spectator uses the red-backed deck while the magician uses the blue-backed deck. Explain to the spectator that if each of you handles his deck in the same way, each of you should arrive at the same conclusion. Emphasize that the spectator is to do exactly what you do.

The magician shuffles his pack. The spectator does likewise. Each person then cuts his own deck. As you square up your deck, glimpse the bottom card. This becomes your Key Card. Of course the glimpse is done secretly.

Now exchange decks with the spectator. He has the blue-backed deck and you have the red-backed deck. Hold the deck in the left hand. Have the spectator do likewise with his pack. Then each of you reaches into the center of his respective deck and removes a card. Tell the spectator to look at his card. You pretend to look at your card.

Each person places his selected card on top of his own deck. Then each person cuts his own deck and completes the cut. Now you exchange decks again. The spectator gets back the red-backed deck and you get the blue-backed deck. Each person turns his own deck face-up so that he alone can see the faces of the cards. Each person then removes his card from the deck he holds. In fact, what you do is locate your original Key Card. Take the card immediately below it and place this card face-down on the table. The spectator does likewise with his deck.

Say, "If we both did the same thing, we should both arrive at the same result." Have the spectator turn over his card so the audience can see it. Then turn over your card. Under the strictest test conditions, using two borrowed well-shuffled decks, it is seen that both you and the spectator have chosen exactly the same card, an amazing coincidence.

23. THE ONE-DECK VERSION

There may be times when two contrasting decks are not available. If you wish to present the basic effect with a single deck, the following method will fill the bill.

Before presenting the trick, remove two cards of the

same value and color, say the 4D and the 4H, and place them on the bottom of the deck. When ready to present the trick, place the deck face-down on the table. Ask the spectator to cut off the top half and keep that half for himself. You take the bottom half.

It is assumed that you are seated at the table across from the spectator. Each person places his half of the deck under the table. Tell the spectator to remove any card from his packet and hand it under the table to you. As soon as he gives you the card, place it on top of your packet. Then immediately ask, "Did you get a good look at your card?" He will say no. Remove the bottom card of your packet and hand it to him. Tell him to look at it and hand it back to you.

Take the card (it will be a red Four) and place it face-up in the middle of your face-down packet. Now remove the bottom card of your packet and hand it under the table to the spectator. Tell him to turn it face-up and place it in the middle of his face-down packet.

When this has been done, both packets are placed face-down to show that the reversed card in the center of each is a red Four.

24. CHILD'S PLAY

In this trick you have two spectators pick cards. The cards are different, but they end up in the same position in two separate packets.

From a well-shuffled deck a spectator is asked to deal two equal heaps of cards. It makes no difference how many cards are dealt so long as each heap contains the same number of cards.

We'll refer to the heaps as "A" and "B" as shown in Figure 16. Ask the spectator to pick up heap "A," shuffle the cards and then note the face (bottom) card of the packet and return the packet to the table in a face-down condition.

Another spectator is asked to remove a few cards

Figure 16

from heap "B," mix the cards and note the face card of the small group. He then places this small group on top of heap "A."

The combined heap at "A" is then dropped on top of whatever cards remain at "B," and the complete packet squared. Now ask for the number of cards originally dealt into either heap. If 12 cards were originally dealt into each heap, deal 12 cards off the combined packet and place the dealt packet at "A."

The undealt portion is turned face-up and placed on the table at position "B." Explain to the audience that because the spectators chose cards in a similar way, they tend to act in sympathy. This is another way of saying that if two people handle cards in the same way, the outcome should be the same.

Deal cards simultaneously from both heaps. When one of the chosen cards shows up as it is dealt from the face-up heap, the spectator who selected this card is requested to call stop. Pause dramatically, then turn over the card you just dealt from the other heap. It will be the other spectator's chosen card.

25. UNSEEN POWERS

Although stemming from a straightforward premise, this routine of J. Stewart Smith's uses a deceptively simple method to bring about a very strong coincidence effect. As a preliminary to the trick, have the four deuces on top of the deck in any order. Place the deck face-down on the table. Ask the spectator to cut the deck into two heaps, which we'll call "A" and "B." Assume that heap "A" is the original top half of the deck.

Pick up heap "A" and place it face-down in the left hand. Deal the top five cards off the top, tossing them out onto the table in different spots. The dealing should look haphazard, but in fact remember where you deal the fifth card.

Place heap "A" beside heap "B" again. Then pick up the last card you dealt, turn it face-up and hand it to the spectator. Tell him to tap each of the other four cards scattered on the table, and to stop on one card. When he decides on a card, leave that card on the table. Gather the remaining cards and place them on top of heap "A." Then take the card the spectator used to tap the other cards, and place this on heap "A." The only single card on the table at this point is the one chosen by the spectator.

Tell him to turn heap "B" face-up. Have him insert his card face-down in the middle of heap "B." Then tell him to hold heap "B" for safekeeping. When he has done this, and his card is securely hidden in the middle of heap "B," pick up heap "A" and say that you too will choose a card. Spread heap "A" face-up between your hands, so that only you can see the faces of these cards. You know that the spectator chose a deuce, but as yet you don't know which one.

As you spread the cards with the faces toward you, note which deuce is missing. Then pick the deuce of the same color and remove it from the packet. For example, if you note that the Two of Diamonds is missing, pick the other red Two, the Two of Hearts, and remove it from the packet.

Close up the packet and turn it face-up. Place your card face-down in the center of this packet. Then have the spectator turn both packets face-down and spread them out. In each packet there will be a face-up card, and each will be a red Two.

26. DOUBLE DISCLOSURE

The only thing needed in this version of the two-deck card trick is a pack of 52 cards. Two spectators participate. The magician never touches the deck, yet the two freely chosen cards end up at identical positions in two separate packets.

So that each spectator has the same number of cards to work with, request the spectator holding the deck to deal off 26 cards and give them to the second spectator. When this has been done, each spectator holds exactly half the deck.

Request each spectator to shuffle his own cards. Then have each person remember the top card of his half of the deck. One half is then placed on top of the other half of the pack. The assembled deck is then given a cut and the cut completed. The deck may be cut several times to insure that no one could possibly know the location of any card.

When the spectator is satisfied that no one knows any card in the deck, he counts 26 cards off the top of the deck, counting them one at a time into a heap on the table. He then places the balance of the deck on the table. One of the packets is chosen, and this packet is turned face-up.

Each spectator takes a packet. They simultaneously deal cards from the top of their respective packets (of course the spectator with the face-up packet is dealing cards off the *face* of his packet, while the spectator with the face-down packet is dealing off the *top* of his packet). When either spectator sees his card being dealt from the face-up heap, he calls stop. The card just dealt from the other heap is turned over and it proves to be the second spectator's chosen card.

27. ULTRA COINCIDENCE

We'll close this chapter with one of the most amazing versions of the two-deck card trick, created by Martin Gardner. A double matching effect is achieved by the most economical means possible.

Two decks are used, one red-backed and one blue-backed. The spectator is asked to pick either deck. Assume he picks the red-backed deck. He shuffles this deck while you shuffle the blue-backed deck. Glance at the bottom card of his deck after he has finished shuffling. (If you are unable to do this, remember the bottom card of your deck and trade decks with him before starting.)

We will assume that the card on the bottom of his deck, the one you glimpsed, is the 3H. Instruct the spectator to remove any card from his deck and place it on top of his deck. You pretend to do the same with your pack. Actually you look for the 3H and place it on top of your deck.

Tell him to place his deck behind his back, cut the deck and complete the cut. You place your deck behind your back and pretend to do the same thing. Actually you do nothing. The 3H is still on top of your deck.

Exchange decks with the spectator. Then have him look through the pack given to him and find his chosen card. You look through the deck he gave you and pretend to look for your card. Actually you look for the Three of Hearts. When you find it, cut it to the top of the pack.

Now remove the top card of your deck and place it face-down on the table. Place the deck to the left of it. Instruct the spectator to place his chosen card face-down on the table and his deck to the left of it. Say to him, "It's easy for me to learn the name of your card. All I have to do is look at the top card of my deck."

Turn up the top card of your deck. Then turn over his chosen card and show that both have matched, as in Figure 17.

"Of course you can learn the name of my card by following the same procedure," the magician adds.

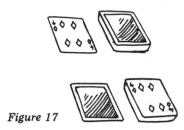

Figure 17

The top card of the spectator's deck is turned face-up. Then the magician's chosen card is turned face-up, and both cards are found to be identical!

Other variations of this classic trick include developments where the bottom card of the spectator's deck is found to match the bottom card of the magician's deck. However, it has been the author's experience that the double climax described above is strong enough to make it one of the most outstanding card effects you will perform.

MENTAL MAGIC
WITH CARDS

Interest in paranormal feats has always been high, and because of the upsurge of interest in magic generally, there has been a dramatic increase in the attention shown toward mentalism. The mentalist has one thing going for him that the magician does not; whereas tricks are generally accepted as clever sleight-of-hand, mentalism is assumed to be *real* magic. Thus, if you present a mental effect as a demonstration of supernormal ability, the audience will not look for sleight-of-hand because they assume there is none to be found anyway.

The present chapter and the one titled "Test Conditions" exploit themes in the area of mental magic, telepathy, prophecy, direct mind control, and so on. Presented as demonstrations or experiments in the unknown, they will be accepted as real magic by almost any audience.

28. THE CARD REVEALED

Before performing this trick, note the top and bottom card of the deck. We will say the top card is the Four of Spades and the bottom card the Jack of Clubs. Hand the deck to the spectator and turn your back.

Ask him to think of a number from 1 to 13. He deals that many cards off the top of the deck, notes the last card dealt, and replaces the dealt packet on top of the pack. Then he gives the deck a cut and completes the cut.

Take back the deck and run through the cards with the faces toward you. Spot the two Key Cards (the Four

of Spades and Jack of Clubs in our example). Count the
number of cards between them and add 1 to this number.
The result may be 8. This tells you that the spectator
originally thought of the number 8.

Now cut the deck so that the Key Card that was
originally on the bottom is back on the bottom of the
pack. Again using our example, the Jack of Clubs, the
original bottom card, would be cut to the bottom of the
deck. This leaves the spectator's chosen card on top of the
pack, but you do not reveal this fact yet.

Since the spectator thought of the number 8, look
through the pack, remove two Eights and place them face-
down on the table side by side. Say to the spectator, "I
can't decide what number you were thinking of, but I'm
almost certain it was one of the numbers represented on
these cards. Fate will guide us to the right choice."

Have the spectator pass his hand over each card and
finally decide on one. Pick up the other one and bury it in
the deck. Then ask him for his thought-of number. It will
be 8. Have him turn over the card he chose and it too will
be an 8-spot.

Then ask, "Now we come to the hard part. What card
did you choose?" After the spectator names it, turn over
the top card of the deck and it will be his chosen card.
This routine was a favorite of J. W. Sarles, and it is his
presentation which is described.

29. THE HAUNTED NAME

"Centuries ago a man named Johan Junius, mistaken-
ly believed to be possessed by demons, was burned at the
stake. His name became associated with mystic phenomena, and his initials still possess strange powers." With this
as background, you perform the following demonstration.
Have the deck shuffled and cut. When you take it back,
glimpse the bottom card. Place the deck on your outstretched palm. Have a spectator remove a group of cards
from the middle of the deck, shuffle them and place them

on top of the deck. Then ask the spectator to write a large
"J" on the back of the top card, to indicate the initial of
Johan Junius' first name.

When he has done this, ask him to cut the deck and
complete the cut. Invite him to cut the deck several more
times. Taking back the deck, spread it face-up on the table
from left to right. Spot your Key Card, the original bottom card you glimpsed. Then remove the card immediately
to the right of this card and mark a large "J" on its face to
indicate the last initial in the name Johan Junius.

Return this card to the deck, square the deck and give
it several cuts. Have the spectator spread the deck face-
down on the table. Let him remove the card bearing the
"J" that he wrote. When he turns this card face-up, he
finds the "J" that you wrote!

30. THOUGHT SPELLER

A spectator is given a packet of cards and asked to
merely think of one of the cards and then mentally spell
out the name of the card. The packet is replaced on top of
the deck and the deck dropped into the magician's pocket.

Turning to another spectator, the magician asks that
person to merely think of his or her lucky number. The
magician removes cards from his pocket one at a time
while the spectator mentally counts to his number. When
he reaches the number, he calls stop.

The magician removes the next card from his pocket
(a spectator can even do it since there is no secret move
made) and the first spectator's thought-of card is discovered. Thus, a card merely thought of by one party is found
at a number merely thought of by another party!

Method: The secret is simple but well concealed. On
top of the deck is a small stack of cards. From the top
down the stack reads: Five of Diamonds, Three of Diamonds, Six of Clubs, Ten of Spades, Eight of Clubs, Queen
of Hearts.

Remove this packet of six cards from the top of the

deck without disturbing the order of the set-up. Hand the packet to the spectator. While your back is turned, he fans the cards so he can see the faces, and he thinks of any card in the packet. When he has done this, have him close up the packet, turn it face-down and hold it in his left hand.

Now instruct him to mentally spell out his card, but as he does so, he is to transfer a card at a time from top to bottom of the packet, transferring one card for each letter. If he thought of the Three of Diamonds, for example, he would spell T – H – R – E – E – D – I – A – M – O – N – D – S, transferring a card for each letter from the top to the bottom of the packet.

When he has done this, have him drop the packet back on top of the deck and square the deck. Take the deck and place it in your pocket. Unknown to all those present, the thought-of card is now on top of the deck. It would be too obvious to merely reach into the pocket and produce the thought-of card, so you disguise the revelation in the following way.

Ask another spectator to think of his or her favorite number. Explain that you will remove cards one at a time from the pocket; the spectator is to stop you when you have counted out a number of cards equal to the favorite number.

Reach into the pocket and begin removing cards one at a time from the *bottom* of the deck, placing each on the table. Continue removing cards until the spectator calls stop. Then remove the *top* card of the deck, bring it out of the pocket and show it to be the chosen card.

31. THE DUPLEX MIND

The secret to the success of most tricks lies in the degree of mystery evoked during the routine. Of themselves, cards are everyday objects and therefore lack mystic or mysterious properties. But you can still use cards in a dramatic context by introducing a mystic-seeming amulet or odd coin. Such objects can be picked up at a modest sum from antique shops or stores catering to coin collectors. The following routine demonstrates how an amulet can be made to seem the center of attention of the mystery, whereas, in fact, its presence in terms of method is mere window-dressing.

Before beginning the routine, arrange to have the Ace of Clubs on top of the deck and the Ace of Spades on the bottom. Any two cards can be used, but it is easy to remember the black Aces.

Now remove the amulet from your pocket and patter about its psychometric properties, its ability to focus thoughts and anything else you can think of that will add to the air of mystery.

Turn your back. Ask spectator "A" to cut off about half of the deck and turn it face-up on the table. Have him note the card he cut to.

In Figure 18, spectator "A" would note the face card of the packet on the left, in this case the Three of Diamonds.

A   B

Figure 18

Ask another spectator to look at the top card of the other half of the deck (packet "B" in Figure 18) and replace this card face-down on top of Packet "B."

Now ask spectator "B" to shuffle the face-up half of the deck into the face-down half. When he has riffle-shuffled the two halves together, tell him to give the deck a cut and complete the cut.

Turn around and face the audience. Pick up the amulet and remark, "While you were selecting cards, the amulet acted as silent observer to your actions. Though it cannot speak, it remembers what it saw and can sometimes convey this information to me."

Spread the deck on the table from left to right. The

audience will see a completely random mixture of face-up and face-down cards. Hold the amulet at the fingertips and pass it over the spread of cards. When you spot the Ace of Clubs, note the first face-up card to the *left* of it. This will be the first spectator's card. Do not hesitate or give any indication that you know the chosen card. Instead, shake your head and say, "I'm picking up a faint vibration. Perhaps it will work better if we turn the deck the other way."

Note that you already know the first spectator's card but you delay revealing this fact. Instead you act just the opposite, as if you do *not* know the card and hope you'll have better luck with the deck facing the other way. Scoop up the deck, turn it over, and spread it on the table from left to right.

As you slowly move the amulet over the cards, spot the position of the Ace of Spades. The first face-up card to the *right* of this Ace will be the card chosen by the second spectator. When your hand passes over this card, allow the amulet to fall onto the deck. Say, "The amulet was drawn to the Nine of Clubs (or whatever the second spectator's card happens to be). Did either of you choose that card?"

One of the spectators will acknowledge that he chose the Nine of Clubs. At this point hand the amulet to the other spectator and say, "The impression of your card is still weak. Perhaps you did not direct your full concentration to your card. Hold the amulet while you concentrate on the card."

Give him a few seconds to concentrate, then take back the amulet and hold it on your outstretched palm. Nod and say, "I'm beginning to see the card now. A red card, wasn't it?" You then go on to name the first spectator's card.

32. PRE-FIGURED

This is another example of the "Lazy Magician" theme discussed elsewhere in this book. In this case, how-

ever, the spectator does all the work and succeeds in revealing the identity of *two* cards.

Tell the spectator that you are going to think of a
card whose identity he is to reveal later. Run through the
deck and remove any 3-spot, say the Three of Spades. Do
not let the spectator see the card you chose; after you
remove it from the deck, place it face-down in the center
of the table.

Now hand him the deck and tell him to think of a
card also. It can be any card except a picture card. When
he has removed his card, place the deck aside and hand the
spectator a pencil and pad of paper.

Instruct him to write down on the pad the value of
his chosen card. Then instruct him to double this number.
If he chose the 9C for instance, he would write the number
18 on the pad. Tell him to add 2 to the result, multiply the
total by 5, and subtract 7 from the final number.

He announces the final number, which might be 93.
Then turn over his card to reveal that it is a 9, and turn
over your card to show that it is a 3, exactly matching the
final number.

33. THREE ON A MATCH

This trick starts out as a serious demonstration of
mind-reading under relatively strict test conditions, but
then it takes an unexpected turn with an amusing finish.

Tell the audience you would like the assistance of
three spectators for an experiment in telepathy. As the
three assisting spectators step forward, pick up the deck
and spread the cards so that only you can see the faces.
Remove seven red cards and place them face-down in a
heap on the table. Then remove a black card and place it
face-down on top of the heap.

Place the deck to one side as it will not be needed.
Then pick up the eight-card packet and hand it to the first
spectator. Explain that he and the other two spectators
will choose cards by a purely random procedure. With the

cards in his own hands, he places the top card on the bottom of the packet, the next card onto the table, the next card under the packet, and so on, until he has one card remaining in his hand.

Tell him to look at and remember this card. He then places it face-down on top of the packet that lies on the table. The cards are squared and this eight-card packet given to the second spectator. He uses the same elimination shuffle to arrive at a random selection. When he has noted his card, he drops it on top of the tabled packet.

The packet is passed to the third spectator. He too uses the same elimination shuffle to arrive at his selection. When he has noted his card, he places it on top of the packet. Then he picks up the packet and gives it a good mixing so that no one knows any of the cards.

Play up the fact that you have not touched the cards from start to finish. Explain that you will now try to find the three chosen cards by purely telepathic means. All that is required, you add, is concentration and the ability to find those cards which appear to stand out from the others.

The spectator holding the packet is asked to deal the cards into a face-up row on the table. When he has dealt out all eight cards, say, "Now all I have to do is find those cards which seem different from the others." The situation should get a laugh because there is *one* and only one card which is different from the rest—the lone black card in the midst of a packet of red cards. At first pretend you do not notice this rather odd situation. Then slowly push the one black card out and place the balance of the packet aside.

Act puzzled that there is only one such card. Then have each of the three spectators name his card. They should be surprised to discover that each of them chose the same card, and in all three cases it was the lone black card!

34. COMPUTER MIND

Years ago Bob Hummer devised a card effect in which the magician was able to reveal a card merely thought of by a spectator. As time went by a number of clever improvements were suggested to the original trick. The following version, devised by Ray Grismer, is one of the best.

As mentioned, this is a method of determining a card merely thought of by a spectator. To perform it you must secretly note the bottom card of the deck and the card second from the top.

When this preparation has been accomplished, give the deck to the spectator and tell him to *think* of any card. Turn your back and tell him that if he thought of a Club or a Heart, he is to deal *one* card onto the table and drop the deck on top. If the thought-of card was a Spade or a Diamond, he does not deal any cards. Remember this first step as "Round One."

Now tell the spectator that if his card was red to deal two cards onto the table. If his card was black, he is to deal three cards. When this has been done, he is to drop the deck onto the cards he dealt onto the table and carefully square up the deck. Remember this as "Round Two."

Now tell the spectator to deal onto the table a number of cards equal to the *value* of the thought-of card. When he has done this, he drops the deck onto the tabled packet and again carefully squares up all cards.

Take the deck from the spectator at this point. Turn it face-up and run the cards singly from left to right so you can see the faces. Recall that in the beginning of the trick you secretly glimpsed the bottom card and the card second from the top. Beginning at the face of the deck, push cards over to the right. Mentally count the number of cards you have to deal *before* you reach the first Key Card (the original bottom card of the deck). Then count the number of cards *between* the first and the second Key Cards. This is all the information you need to reveal the identity of the spectator's thought-of card.

The number of cards *between* the Key Cards gives you the suit of the thought-of card as follows:

Clubs   3 cards
Hearts   2 cards
Spades   1 card
Diamonds   no cards

Now that you know the suit, you can determine the value of the thought-of card. If the thought-of card was a Club or a Heart, the number of cards before the first Key Card *is* the value of the thought-of card.

On the other hand, if the thought-of card was a Spade or a Diamond, subtract one from the number of cards before the first Key, and this is the identity of the spectator's thought-of card.

35. THE STOP TRICK

The secret to this trick, credited to Annemann, was at one time sold in a manuscript costing $50. In effect a spectator's card is found by means of a number merely *thought of* by another spectator.

The top 13 cards of the deck are stacked. From the top down the set-up is K – Q – J – 10 – 9 – 8 – 7 – 6 – 5 – 4 – 3 – 2 – A. The King is the top card of the deck. Remove the Joker from the deck, turn it face-up and place it on the bottom of the deck.

To perform the trick, spread the deck between the hands and have a card chosen from the center of the deck. While the spectator shows the card to the others present, secretly count off thirteen cards from the top of the deck. Lift these cards off as a packet and have the spectator's card returned. Then place this packet on top of his card. Square up the deck. Then cut the deck and complete the cut. Tell him that his card will be found by means of a number thought of by another spectator. As you talk, casually cut the deck two or three times. Then pretend to notice that there is a card accidentally reversed in the deck. Spread the deck until you come to the face-up Joker. Cut the deck at that point so the Joker is the top card. Remove it from the deck, saying, "The Joker shouldn't be in the deck anyway."

Now have someone think of a number from 1 to 10. Ask him to name his number. If it is 9, slowly count nine cards off the top of the deck. Ask him if he wants the last card you counted or the next one on top of the deck. If he says the next one, turn that card face-up. Whatever number shows on this card, count that many cards further into the deck. The last card you count will be the chosen card.

36. SENSITIVE FINGERTIPS

In this routine, the invention of Jack Avis, the magician is given a shuffled deck of cards behind his back. Without looking at any cards, and by means of his super-sensitive fingertips, the magician is able to "read" the values of the cards one at a time while they are behind his back. In a final test, the magician reveals the names of two more cards while the deck is in the spectator's hands.

Figure 19

Method: Six cards are secretly removed from the deck and hidden under the belt in back. These six cards will be the AC – 4H – 7S – 10D – 8S – KC, in that order from top to bottom. Figure 19 shows how they are clipped under the belt. They may also be held in place with a large paper clip, or kept in the back pocket, but for ease of handling, it is recommended that the packet be clipped under the belt as shown.

Have the balance of the deck shuffled by the spectator. Take it behind your back. Remove the packet from under the belt and add it to the top of the deck. Tell the audience about your supersensitive fingertips. Pretend to rub the fingers on the top card of the deck. Say, "This feels like an Ace, possibly a black Ace. Yes, it's the Ace of Clubs." Bring out the top card and show that it is the Ace of Clubs.

Repeat the same procedure for the second card, naming the Four of Hearts, then bringing it out and tossing it onto the table. For the third card, do *not* name the Seven of Spades. Name the Eight of Spades, but bring out the Seven of Spades. Quickly flash the face of this card, but do not give the audience time to study the face.

Tell the spectator you will try a more difficult feat. Have him cut the deck and complete the cut. Now pick up the face-down Seven of Spades, call it the Eight of Spades again, and put it on top of the deck. Then have the spectator cut the deck and complete the cut to bury this card.

Now tell him to step away and remove the card on either side of the Eight of Spades. When he has done this, pretend to concentrate, and then reveal that these cards are the Ten of Diamonds and the King of Clubs.

37. THINK OF AN ACE

Beforehand arrange the Aces in the deck as follows: the Ace of Clubs about 10th down from the top, the Ace of Hearts about 20th from the top, the Ace of Spades 30th from the top and the Ace of Diamonds 40th from the top.

When ready to present the routine, hand the spectator the deck and remark on the fact that the Aces, because they represent the highest cards in the deck, have a fascination about them that other cards do not have. To illustrate, ask the spectator to think of an Ace. Tell him to fan the cards so he can see the faces, find the thought-of Ace, and upjog it slightly so he can see the face of the card.

As you talk, walk away from the spectator so your back is turned to him. Remove another deck from your pocket and say that you too will think of an Ace. Just as you say this, turn and face the spectator, and note the approximate position of the upjogged Ace in his deck. Of course you will see only the backs of the cards in his deck, but with very little practice you should be able to judge immediately whether his thought-of card protrudes from the deck near the top (in which case it would be the Ace of Clubs), nearer to the center (the Ace of Hearts), about two-thirds of the way down from the top (the Ace of Spades) or near the bottom (the Ace of Diamonds).

While this may sound difficult at first reading, it is an easy knack to pick up. In time you will be able to judge the approximate location of the upjogged Ace by the merest glance. Thus, the audience will never remember that you turned back to look at all.

Once you have spotted the position of the upjogged Ace, and hence know its identity, turn your back to the spectator. Run through your deck and remove the same Ace. Hold it over your head, with the back of the card to the spectator.

Have him remove his card from his own deck. Both of you then show your chosen Ace to the audience, and it is seen that the Aces are identical. In performing this trick you will find that a curious "aftereffect" develops. When describing the trick later on, people will forget that the choice was restricted to the four Aces; instead they will swear that the fellow from the audience chose any card and that you matched it in some miraculous manner.

38. POCKET PREDICTION

This is an adaptation of a first-rate trick credited to Rufus Steele. Tell the spectator that you will try to predict a card he is going to choose. To make sure there is no tampering with the prediction, tell him that you will give him the card to hold.

Taking a borrowed, well-shuffled deck from the spectator, turn the cards face-up so that you alone can see the faces. Spot the top card of the deck. We will say it is a 9-spot. Silently count in to the 9th card from the face of the deck, and note this card. It may be the Five of Spades.

Find the "twin" of the Five of Spades, in other words, the other black Five. Remove this card from the deck and hand it face-down to the spectator as your prediction. Tell him to place it in his pocket for safekeeping.

Now turn the deck face-up and begin dealing cards one at a time off the face into a face-up heap on the table. Continue dealing until you have dealt past the Five of Spades, then say to the spectator, "Call stop at any time."

When he calls stop, pick up the face-up packet from the table, turn it face-down and place it in front of the spectator. Tell him that he will choose a card from this packet.

Now turn the balance of the deck face-down in your hand and begin dealing cards off the top. Tell the spectator to call stop at any time. When he does, pick up the tabled packet you have just dealt, turn it face-up and point to the face card of the packet. Say to the spectator, "This card is a 9-spot, so count down to the 9th card in your packet."

The spectator counts to the 9th card and turns it face-up. It will be the Five of Spades. "You chose a black Five," you remark. "Now check this against the prediction card I gave you before we began the trick."

The spectator removes the prediction card from his pocket and finds that it is the other black Five, a perfect match.

39. PSYCHIC MAGNET

Tell a spectator that certain cards have an affinity for certain objects. For example, you say, the Two of Spades is magnetic and is easily attracted by a magnet. To illustrate, you hold a deck of cards in your hand, and throw a handkerchief over the deck. A borrowed pencil, suitably charged by a psychic field, is held over the deck, and the Two of Spades immediately rises out of the deck, clinging to the pencil as if it were in fact responding to some kind of magnetic field. All objects may be borrowed, and all may be left with the spectator at the finish of the demonstration.

Method: Shuffle and cut the deck. As you square up the cards, glimpse the top card of the deck. If it is the Two of Spades, then this is the card you mention as being peculiarly susceptible to psychic magnetism.

Hand someone a pencil. Tell him to gaze at it and imagine it is a solid ferrite magnet. As he does this, cover the deck with a handkerchief. A light silk handkerchief works best, but a cotton or linen handkerchief is also suitable.

Take the pencil and hold it over the deck. Touch the top of the deck with it. Do not be in a hurry to perform the trick. The longer you delay, the more "genuine" the experiment appears. After trying it two or three times without success, hand the pencil back to the spectator and ask him and one or two other spectators to concentrate harder on making the pencil magnetic. While attention is directed to the spectators and the pencil, secretly moisten the tip of your right little finger.

Take the pencil again and place it on top of the deck. Then, behind the cover afforded by the silk, push the little finger against the handkerchief so it comes in contact with the top card of the deck. Then lift the right hand slowly, all the while maintaining pressure, and the card will "rise" out of the deck as if magnetically attracted to the pencil; see Figure 20. The key to making this a convincing demonstration of psychic magnetism is to focus all attention on the pencil and not on the cards.

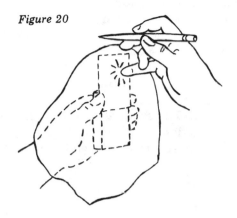

Figure 20

40. FATE #1

Cards and dice are articles common to many gambling games, yet they are seldom used together in the same game. The reason (you explain) is that when used in conjunction with one another, they produce strange, sometimes unexpected results. To demonstrate, you use two dice and a deck of cards. The dice can be shaken in a leather dice cup if such an item is available, but otherwise the two dice may be shaken in a teacup or other opaque container.

The spectator shakes the dice and tosses them out onto the table. Whatever number shows up on the dice, the spectator deals that many cards from the top of the deck into a packet on the table.

The spectator then turns either die over and notes the new top number. Whatever it is, the spectator counts that many additional cards off the deck and onto the packet already on the table. The deck itself is placed aside at this point.

Calling attention to the other die, the one not turned over, the magician calls out the top number and requests that the spectator count that many cards off the top of the packet into a separate heap on the table.

There are two small packets of cards on the table. "Isn't it odd," the magician remarks, "that the random throw of the dice gave you just the right cards needed to open a game of draw poker?" So saying, he turns over the top card of each small packet, revealing a pair of Jacks!

Method: Beforehand, arrange two black Jacks so they are 6th and 7th from the top of the deck. Then simply proceed as described above. Regardless of the numbers thrown by the spectator, the end result will always be a pair of Jacks.

41. FATE #2

This is a different version of the above trick. The patter story is the same. The spectator rolls two dice and totals the top numbers. Whatever the total, he counts that many cards off the top of the deck into a face-down heap on the table.

The spectator then covers one of the dice with the cup. This leaves the other die in view. Direct the spectator to turn this die over so the bottom number is now on top. Have him note the new number and deal this many additional cards onto the packet already on the table.

Remark on the fact that the spectator rolled a completely random number with the two dice. Point out also that one die is still hidden under the cup, its identity known only to the spectator. "But such is the sympathy that exists between cards and dice," you add, "that one card was fated to be dealt."

Turn up the top card of the packet on the table. It will be a Five. Then have the cup lifted from the die. The top number on the die is also seen to be a Five, a perfect match.

Method: Arrange the Ace, Two, Three, Four, Five, Six in mixed suits on top of the deck in numerical order, Ace at the top, Six on the bottom. With this packet on top of the deck, you proceed with the trick exactly as written above. It will always turn out that the last card the spectator deals matches in value the top face of the die hidden under the cup.

42. DOUBLE PROPHET

Two cards chosen in the fairest possible manner with the deck in the spectator's own hands are found to match two predictions written by the performer and sealed in envelopes before the demonstration began.

To make the predictions as impressive as possible, write on a slip of paper, "You will pick the 8H and also. . . ." Don't complete the prediction. Instead, fold it in half, drop it in an envelope, seal the envelope and mail it to yourself. On a second slip of paper, write ". . . and also the Queen of Clubs." Fold this prediction in half, drop it into a separate envelope, seal the envelope and mail it to yourself.

You will thus have two sealed envelopes, each containing part of the double prediction, and each clearly sealed and officially dated prior to the evening you intend to perform the trick.

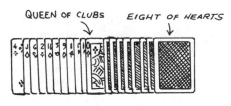

Figure 21

On the night you do the trick, secretly perform the following preparation. Place the Eight of Hearts on top of the deck and the Queen of Clubs on the bottom. Then turn the bottom half of the deck around so it is face to face with the top half of the deck. Figure 21 shows the condition of the deck and the relative position of the two prediction cards at this point.

To perform the trick, hand the deck to the spectator and tell him to place it behind his back. The top card of the deck is the face-down Eight of Hearts at this point.

With the deck behind his back the spectator is instructed to lift off about a quarter of the deck and turn it face up on top of the pack. When he has done this, tell him to lift off about two-thirds of the deck and turn it over onto the balance of the deck. When he's done this, take the deck from him.

Spread the cards from left to right, saying that you will use the last face-down card near the top of the deck and the first face-down card near the center of the deck. As you begin spreading the deck you will first come across a group of face-down cards. Run through these until you come to the last face-down card in the top group. Upjog this card. It is shown as "A" in Figure 22.

Figure 22

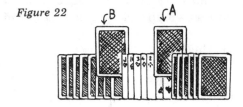

You will next encounter a group of face-up cards. Push these to the right until you come to the first face-down card of the next group. Upjog this card. It is shown as "B" in Figure 22. Square up the deck and remove the two upjogged cards. Then call attention to the two sealed envelopes that you previously placed on the table. Have the first one read aloud. Then explain that the second prediction came in the mail a day after the first. Have the second envelope opened and the prediction read aloud. It is seen that both of the chosen cards have been correctly predicted.

If you want to make the predictions more impressive, burn each prediction slip around the edges and sign each, "Beelzebub." You can later explain that while it is true

Beelzebub is referred to as the prince of demons, he is also a good golfer (a 3 handicap), and rather talented at writing predictions when he is not out on the golf course raising— er, heck. You then proceed with the above trick.

TEST CONDITIONS

Like the last chapter, this chapter deals with mental effects, but there is a difference. Here we will consider those routines which are done under seemingly rigid test conditions, where—even if the spectator suspects the possibility of chicanery—it would appear impossible for the demonstration to succeed.

43. BLIND DICE #1

The first part of this routine is adapted from a trick associated with Kuda Bux. The second part ("Blind Dice #2") is a variation suggested by the author. Needed is any deck of cards and dice, two for the first part, three for the second.

Have the deck thoroughly shuffled and cut by the spectator. Remove two dice from your pocket and toss them onto the table. While you turn around or leave the room, the spectator rolls the two dice and adds together the two top numbers. If these are, for example, a 6 and a 3, the spectator would remember the total 9. Then one of the dice is turned over and the new number added to the total. Thus, if the new number were a 4, the total thus far would be 13. Finally, the spectator picks up this same die and rolls it. Whatever number comes up is added; if the number that came up were a 5, the grand total would be 18.

The spectator then notes a card at a corresponding

position down in the deck. In our example, the spectator would note the 18th card from the top of the deck.

The magician turns around, picks up the deck and immediately finds the chosen card.

Method: When you turn around to take the deck, glance at the two dice on the table. Mentally add their numbers together, then add 7 to the result. This automatically tells you the location of the spectator's card in the deck. In our case you would arrive at a total of 18, and would go on to remove the 18th card from the top of the deck. If the audience asks to see the trick again, proceed with the following variation.

44. BLIND DICE #2

Add a third die to the two dice on the table, saying that this will make it a bit harder. Turn your back. The spectator rolls the three dice and adds together the top faces. Then any two dice are turned over and the new numbers on top added to the remembered total. Finally, one of these two dice is pocketed by the spectator. The other die of the two dice is thrown at random, and the number thrown on this die is added to give the spectator a grand total which he alone knows.

He looks at a card at a position from the top of the deck which corresponds to the grand total. The magician, who may be out of the room until this point, takes the deck and instantly finds the chosen card.

Method: When you take the deck from the spectator, glance at the two dice on the table. Add together the numbers on top of the two dice. Then add 14 to this to arrive at a grand total. Whatever this total is, it tells you the location of the chosen card in the deck. Thus, if the total is 20, you know the spectator's chosen card is 20th from the top of the deck.

The trick is puzzling because only two of the dice are seen, the third die being hidden in the spectator's pocket.

Although the trick is automatic in operation, do not make it look too easy; pretend to have difficulty getting the proper mental impression, hesitate, change your mind, then finally decide on the right card.

45. HOCUS-POCUS

Three small packets of cards are dealt onto the table. While the magician turns his back, a spectator chooses any one of the packets, shuffles it, mentally decides on one card in the packet, and then shuffles the packet again.

This packet is sandwiched between the other two packets to make sure the mentally chosen card is really buried. Neither the magician nor the spectator knows where the thought-of card is, and of course the magician has no idea of the identity of the thought-of card.

The spectator is asked to deal five heaps of cards from the packet. He is to continue dealing a card to each heap until he has dealt out all of the cards in the packet. Then, while the magician still keeps his back turned, the spectator locates the heap that contains his mentally chosen card, and places this heap in his jacket pocket.

For the first time the magician turns around and faces the spectator. Reviewing the impossibly strict conditions, including the fact that the spectator has shuffled, cut and thought of a card without the magician ever seeing or touching the cards, the magician says he will try to find the spectator's chosen card by a telepathic process known as psychometry. With this process the magician will seek to find the one card in the spectator's pocket which the spectator himself has chosen as his own card.

The magician reaches into the spectator's pocket and immediately withdraws the thought-of card!

Method: This trick, the invention of Eddie Joseph, can be built up to a feat of remarkable powers because the magician in fact never touches the cards nor does he have the slightest idea which card was chosen by the spectator. The key to its success is in the casualness of the handling. You must make it appear that your initial handling of the cards is unimportant. Presented as such, the spectator will promptly forget that the magician ever touched the cards.

When the shuffled deck is handed to you, deal or push off a bunch of cards. It should look like a random number of cards, but in fact the packet must contain five cards exactly. Place this packet on the table. Remove another packet of five cards and drop them on the table. Then remove a final packet of five cards and place them on the table. At this point there will be three heaps of cards on the table, each containing five cards. Again, it must be stressed that you should not appear to be counting the cards or handling them with precision. It must look as if you are dropping three bunches of cards on the table.

From this point on you turn your back and do not handle the cards again. Ask the spectator to pick up one of the packets and shuffle it. Then ask him to look at one of the cards in the packet and remember it. A strong point now is that you ask him to shuffle the packet again so that even he does not know the location of his chosen card.

Tell him to place his packet between the other two packets. Then ask him to deal five heaps of cards. He deals in the conventional way, from left to right, dealing a card at a time to each heap until he has dealt all 15 cards. When he has finished dealing, he will have five heaps on the table, each containing three cards.

Ask him to find the heap containing his thought-of card, and to place this heap in his jacket pocket. When he has done this (your back has been turned all this time), turn around and review the proceedings thus far, emphasizing that you never touched the cards.

Reach into the spectator's pocket and simply take the *center* card of the packet of three. Remove it from the spectator's pocket and dramatically reveal it as the selected card.

46. OUT OF SIGHT

A spectator chooses a card and places it in his pocket. He then shuffles the deck and hands it to the magician. The magician drops the deck into his own pocket and without looking at the cards, he removes one from the deck. The spectator shows the card he chose—the 5D for example. The magician then shows the card he selected while the deck was in his pocket—it is the 5H, the other red Five.

Method: Before the trick begins, place one of the red Fives in your jacket pocket. Then position the other red Five so it lies 10th from the top of the deck. This preparation is done secretly, as you do not want the audience to be aware of this setting-up procedure.

When ready to perform the trick, place the deck face-down in the left hand. Ask the spectator for a number between 10 and 20. Say he names 17. Slowly count 17 cards off the top, one at a time, dealing them into a pile on the table.

After you have dealt the 17 cards, say to the spectator, "To make this even more random, we'll use the two digits in the number 17. Taking 1 and 7, we add them together and arrive at a total of 8." As you talk, pick up the packet of cards you dealt onto the table and replace them on top of the deck. Then deal 8 cards off the top one at a time. Give the 8th card to the spectator and tell him to place it in his pocket for safekeeping.

Instruct the spectator to assemble the deck and shuffle it thoroughly. Then take the deck from him and drop it in your jacket pocket, that is, the pocket which contains the red Five. Pretend to concentrate for a minute, as if trying to fathom the card in the spectator's pocket.

Remove three or four cards from the deck one at a time, and toss them out onto the table. Each time shake your head and say, "No, that's not the one I want." Pause dramatically and say, "I think the next one will be it." Remove the red Five from the pocket and hold it face-down in the hand. Have the spectator remove his chosen card and show it to the audience. Remark that he chose a red Five. Then turn your card over to show that you chose the other red Five.

47. LONG DISTANCE

Astonishing as it may seem, it is possible to perform card tricks over the telephone. This means that the magician, calling from a house that may be a town or a state away from the spectator, can reveal a card chosen by the spectator under conditions that are the most stringent imaginable; not only is the magician away from the deck when the card is being chosen, he may be hundreds or thousands of miles away!

Credit for devising the basic idea of a telephone trick is given to John Northern Hilliard. Over the years many clever minds have devised methods of performing a trick over the telephone. The following presentation, suggested by Audley Walsh, is one of the most impressive.

Call up a friend and explain that you would like to try a test in telepathy over the telephone. Ask him to bring a deck of cards to the phone. When he has done this, ask him to cut the deck into two approximately equal piles.

Then ask him to choose one of the piles and discard the other. He is to shuffle the chosen pile thoroughly. Then tell him to count the cards in this pile.

He will arrive at a two-digit number for his total, but caution him not to tell you the number. Instead, he is to mentally add together the two digits. Then he is to discard from his selected pile the same number of cards as the total of the two digits.

Instruct him to think of a number from 1 to 10, remove that number of cards from the chosen pile, and place them in his pocket. When he has done this, have him count down in the remainder of his selected pile to the same thought-of number and remember the identity of the card that lies at that position in the pile.

Now for the first time you ask him for some information. Tell him to hold his selected pile face-down in his left hand, deal cards one at a time off the top, and name them out loud to you. When he has read off all the cards, you immediately name the card he chose. Then as a topper you tell him the number of cards he has concealed in his pocket.

The method is easy and is never suspected. Before you call the spectator, bring a pad and pencil to the telephone. Instruct the spectator in the handling of the cards exactly as described above. When you reach the point where the spectator begins calling out the names of the cards one at a time, jot them down in a vertical column on the pad.

When he's finished calling out the cards, count the number of cards listed on your pad. Whatever this number is, subtract it from 18. If your result is, for example, 6, then the spectator's chosen card is the 6th one from the beginning of your list, and further, the spectator has exactly six cards in his pocket!

On rare occasions you will find that the spectator will call out more than 18 cards. If he does, then your factor becomes 27; subtract the number of cards he calls out from 27. Then proceed with the remainder of the trick exactly as written above.

48. THE PHONE MIRACLE

This version of the telephone trick was devised by J. G. Thompson, Jr., the brilliant magician/mentalist. If you have performed the preceding trick, "Long Distance," for friends, and are asked at a later date to do the trick again, Mr. Thompson's routine is ideal. It rests on an entirely different premise and will therefore be even more baffling to audiences.

Call up a friend and have him bring a deck of cards to the phone. Ask him to cut off about one quarter of the deck, count the cards in the packet he cut off and deal from the packet two piles of cards: one pile is to contain the same number of cards as the first digit of the total and the second pile is to contain the same number of cards as the second digit of the total.

For example, if he cut off a packet of 14 cards, he would deal one card into the first pile and four cards into the second pile. When he has done this, ask him to shuffle the remaining cards in the packet he cut off the deck and look at the bottom card of this packet. This will be his chosen card. He then replaces the packet on top of the deck.

Finally, he is to gather up the two small piles he dealt (in our example the small piles consist of one card and four cards, respectively) and place them on the bottom of the deck.

Now have a second spectator come to the phone. Tell him to transfer the top card to the bottom of the deck. This signals the deck that you are ready for the thought experiment. Tell him to think of a number between 10 and 20, but not to tell you what it is. Whatever number he has thought of, he is to deal that many cards off the top of the deck into a pile on the table. When this has been done, ask him to place the balance of the deck aside, as it will not be used.

This spectator adds together the two digits of the mentally chosen number. Whatever the result, he deals that many cards off the packet and places them aside. Then from the remainder of the packet he deals the top three cards in a row on the table. Tell him to name the three cards, calling them either from left to right or from right to left, but without telling you which way he is calling them.

Despite the fact that you do not know either number, that you do not ask any questions and that you do not even know if the deck itself is complete, you proceed immediately to name the card chosen by the first spectator.

The secret is remarkably simple. Of the three cards dealt by the second spectator, the center card will always be the chosen card. Thus it does not matter whether the spectator calls out the cards from left to right or right to left; the second card he calls out must be the chosen card in either case.

49. A CARD AND A NUMBER

Properly performed, this is an unfathomable card mystery. The only requirement is that a deck of 52 cards must be used. The effect is one where a card randomly selected by one spectator is made to appear at a position in the deck freely designated by another spectator.

Ask spectator "A" to give the deck several shuffles and cuts. Then ask him to think of a number between 1 and 10. Tell him to remove that many cards from the deck and conceal them in his pocket. In other words, if he thought of the number 6, he would remove six cards from the deck and place them in his pocket.

Then have spectator "A" note the card that lies at the corresponding position from the top of the deck. In our example, spectator "A" would note the card that lies 6th from the top of the pack. All of this is done while the magician has his back turned or is out of the room. He has no idea of the number chosen by spectator "A" and it is this fact which makes the trick so puzzling.

Now explain that you want someone else to name a number. To make certain this number is nowhere near spectator "A's" number, you ask that this number be between 25 and 40. Say that the number 32 is called out.

Tell the audience that you will attempt the impossible by placing "A's" card at a position exactly 32 from the top of the deck. You will do this even though you do not know "A's" card or where it lies. And further, you will do it without looking at the cards.

Place the deck behind your back. Starting at the next number after the one called out, you count cards off the top one at a time, transferring each card to the bottom of the deck. You continue counting until you reach the number 52. In our example, the number called out was 32. You will thus begin your count on the number 33. Transfer cards from top to bottom one at a time, each card corresponding to a number as you count from 33 to 52.

When you have done this, bring the deck back out into view. Again ask for the number called out. Since it is 32 in our example, count cards off the top of the pack, beginning at 1 and continuing until you reach 32. Turn up the last card dealt and it will be the card noted by spectator "A."

50. MAGIC BY PROXY

In this version of the telephone trick, you do not need to make a call. In fact, the telephone is never lifted from the receiver. As the audience sees it, a card is chosen and replaced in the deck. You, the magician, never touch the deck. Then, *without* lifting the phone from the receiver, you dial the number of a psychic friend. You explain that he can receive telephone messages by direct mind reading, a fact which is naturally reflected in a minuscule phone bill at the end of each month.

After you dial his number, you wait about a minute. Then the telephone rings. It rings exactly twice and then stops. A few more seconds go by. The phone begins ringing again. This time it rings three times and then stops.

Turning to the spectator who holds the deck, you say, "The phone rang twice and then three times. This indicates the number 23. Would you count down to the 23rd card in the deck?" The spectator does, and is astonished to find his card at exactly that position in the deck.

Method: The entire working of the trick depends on two things; the first is a brilliant placement idea of Gerald Kosky's and the second is nothing more than a little discussion, before performing the trick, with your friend who is going to play the part of the psychic.

This is how it works. Tell your friend that at ten o'clock on such-and-such a night you are going to perform this trick. He is to ring you at about ten after ten, let the phone ring twice and then hang up. He is then to dial you back immediately, let the phone ring exactly three times and again hang up.

That is all he needs to know. On the appointed evening, at ten o'clock, you mention that you would like to perform an experiment in extrasensory perception. Ask for the loan of a deck of cards. It must contain 52 cards.

You do not touch the deck at any time. Ask a spectator to shuffle the deck. Then tell him to remove a small number of cards—up to 15 cards—count them and drop them in his pocket.

Then tell him to count down from the top of the deck to the same number and remember the card at that number. When he has done this, tell him that there is a certain card in the deck that acts as the mystic link between the spectator's mind and the psychic's. Ask the spectator to deal off the top card, name it and place it on the bottom of the deck.

He is to continue dealing cards off the top one at a time, naming them and placing them on the bottom until you tell him to stop. You pretend to be listening for a particular card, but in fact you mentally count the number of cards he deals and call stop when he has dealt exactly 29 cards from top to bottom.

When he has called out the 29th card—say the Five of Clubs—and placed it on the bottom, suddenly call stop and add, "That's it, the Five of Clubs! All right, we have the psychic link. I can call my friend."

Go to the phone, but do not lift the phone from the cradle. Simply dial any number. Glance at your watch so that you can gauge how close it is to ten after ten. You can stall a bit if you still have a few minutes to wait before your psychic friend calls you back. In any event, at ten after ten the phone will ring twice and then stop. There will be a slight pause; then the phone rings three times and stops.

Ask the spectator to look at the 23rd card from the

top of the deck. Since you never touched the cards, he will be amazed that his card is exactly 23 from the top. Properly performed, this is as dramatic a demonstration of telepathy as you could wish for.

51. SIGNED, SEALED AND DELIVERED

If you know in advance that you will have a chance to perform a few magic tricks at an office party, banquet or any other social function scheduled at least a week in the future, you can take advantage of the occasion to perform a sealed prediction feat that appears to have no solution except genuine telepathy.

Before the evening of the banquet, write on a piece of paper, "The chosen card will be the Seven of Spades." Fold the prediction and seal it in a small envelope. Seal this envelope in a larger envelope. Finally, write a note to the banquet chairman, saying, "On the night of —— [fill in the correct date], please bring the enclosed sealed prediction to the banquet. You may also wish to bring your own deck of cards, because at that time I shall try an experiment in clairvoyance, and wish to observe the strictest test conditions."

Place the sealed prediction and the note to the chairman in an envelope and send the envelope to him. You can call him ahead of time to alert him to the package he is going to receive. Merely ask for his cooperation in keeping the prediction in a well-guarded place until the night of the banquet, to prevent any suspicion of tampering.

On the evening of the banquet, borrow a deck of cards or use one of your own. Have it well shuffled by anyone in the audience. Then take it back and state that you want to be certain the deck does not contain a Joker. Look through the pack for Jokers. In fact, you are looking for the Seven of Spades. Cut the 7S to the top of the deck. If you spot any Jokers in the pack, discard them, but this point is unimportant; your reason for looking through the deck is to get the 7S to the top.

Now hand the face-down deck to the banquet chairman. Ask him to lift off a portion of cards from the top, turn this portion face-up, and place it (still face-up) onto the balance of the deck. When he has done this, ask him to turn the entire deck over, and to spread it from left to right on the table.

Instruct him to remove the first face-down card in the middle of the deck. This will be the face-down card directly to the left of the face-up portion of the deck. Have him show this card to all those present. The card will be the Seven of Spades, an outcome guaranteed by the handling. Then have him open the prediction envelope and read aloud the prediction, verifying that you were 100% correct.

The ingenious method used here to force the Seven of Spades was developed by Lin Searles, and has many applications in card work.

STRANGE SECRETS

When an extra card is added to a deck, this card is known in magical parlance as a Stranger Card. The extra card may or may not have the same back pattern as the deck it is being added to, depending on the application. It is an easy matter to obtain such cards. When buying a deck, simply purchase a second deck of cards which has the same back pattern. You may want to buy two such extra decks, one with the same back pattern and the same color, and one with the same back pattern but with a contrasting-color back. Thus equipped, you will be ready to perform any of the tricks described in this chapter.

52. IMPOSSIBLE LOCATION

The value of a Stranger Card in a card effect is such that it can elevate an otherwise ordinary trick into the miracle category. The following is such an effect; you locate a chosen card under difficult conditions, then proceed to repeat the trick, locating the same card under impossible conditions.

Run through the deck you plan to use and remove any card, say the Nine of Hearts. Place this card in your right jacket pocket. Then remove the duplicate Nine of Hearts from another pack and position this card 10th in from the face of the deck you plan to use. This deck is placed in its case and dropped into the left-hand jacket pocket until you are ready to perform the trick. Note that if the deck you plan to use is blue-backed the duplicate 9H you placed 10th from the face should be red-backed.

To set the stage for the trick, get the conversation around to methods used by card sharpers and the fact that many of them have developed sensitive fingertips to the point where they can locate certain cards in the deck merely by sense of touch alone.

Remove the deck from its case and place it face up on the table. Ask a spectator to give you a number between 10 and 20. He might name 15. You then deal 15 cards off the face of the face-up deck into a heap on the table.

Then tell him that in order to make the number completely arbitrary, you will randomize his number. Pick up the packet you just dealt onto the table and replace it face-up onto the face of the deck. Then say that the number 15 contains two digits, a 1 and a 5. Adding these together, you arrive at the number 6.

Deal 6 cards off the face of the deck. Ask the spectator to remember the last card dealt (it will be the 9H). Then drop the balance of the deck onto the cards that lie on the table.

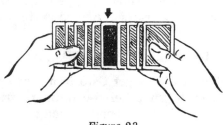

Figure 23

Still keeping the cards face-up, invite the spectator to shuffle the deck several times. When he has done this, take back the deck and turn it face-down. Hold the deck so it is vertical to the floor, with the faces of the cards toward the audience. Say that you will try to find his card without looking at the faces of any card in the deck. As you talk, spread the cards from left to right between the hands. Only you can see the backs of the cards, and when you come upon the Stranger Card it will be readily visible, as in Figure 23.

Pause for dramatic effect, then remove the Stranger Card from the deck and ask if you were correct. The audience will say yes. Still keeping the face of the Stranger Card toward the audience, place this card onto the face or bottom of the deck. Square up the deck and drop it into your left jacket pocket. Then, as an afterthought, say to the audience, "Let me show you that again, under even more impossible conditions." Remove the deck from the pocket but leave the Stranger Card behind in the pocket.

Have the spectator shuffle and cut the deck. Then have him divide it into five or six packets. Pretend to study the packets. Finally pick up one packet and drop it into your *right* jacket pocket. Say that you'll try to find the Nine of Hearts this time without even looking at any cards. Reach into your right jacket pocket and remove the Nine of Hearts previously placed there. Withdraw it from the pocket and bow to the applause.

53. SLIM CHANCE

This is a prediction trick with a twist. The magician's prediction appears to be wrong, but then it is discovered that the prediction was correct and in an unexpected manner.

Preparation consists in having the Stranger Card on the bottom of the deck. For this trick it is best to use a blue-backed deck. The Stranger Card is red-backed, and will be the 9S.

On the prediction slip write, "You will choose a red card." Fold the slip in half and then in quarters and drop it onto the table.

Now have the spectator cut some cards off the top of the deck as shown in Figure 24. We will assume that the packet he has cut off goes to position "A" on the table. The balance of the deck (the original bottom portion of the deck) is shown in position "B" in Figure 24.

Now tell him to turn the top card of packet "B" face-up and place it still face-up on top of packet "A,"

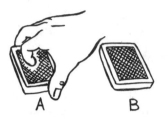

Figure 24

saying that this will mark the place where he cut. When he has done this, have him place packet "B" on top of packet "A."

Take the assembled deck from him and spread it *face-up* on the table from left to right. Point to the location of the reversed card and say, "We'll use the card directly above the reversed card." Remove the card above the reversed card and show it as the 9S. Have the spectator remember this card. Then return it to the deck. Finally, remove the reversed card and place it face-up on the face of the deck.

Say, "Remember that I wrote a prediction before you chose the Nine of Spades." Have the prediction opened and read aloud. It says, "You will choose a red card." When the spectator has finished reading the prediction, frown and ask, "Is that all I wrote?" The prediction is obviously wrong since the spectator chose a black card.

Then snap your fingers and say, "Of course. Now I remember what I had in mind. When I said you would choose a red card, I was referring to the *back* of the card." Spread the deck face-down on the table. In the entire spread of the blue deck the audience sees a single red-backed card. It is removed, turned face-up, and proves to be the spectator's chosen card, the Nine of Spades.

54. THE BLUE PHANTOM

This routine of Roy Walton's cleverly exploits the use of a Stranger Card. Note here that the intervention of the

Stranger Card is delayed so as to bring about a strong finish in an amusing and unexpected manner.

A red-backed deck is used. Remove any card from the deck—say the Ten of Diamonds—and place it aside, as it is not used in this trick. Then remove the duplicate Ten of Diamonds from a blue-backed deck and place it 15 in from the face of the red-backed deck. You are now ready to perform the trick.

Place the pack face-down on the table. Invite spectator "A" to remove a few cards from the top, adding that he should remove fewer than a dozen cards. When he has done this, turn the pack face-up and replace it on the table. Ask spectator "B" to remove fewer than a dozen cards from the face of the deck.

Each spectator now holds a random number of cards. Ask spectator "A" to count the cards he has and to remember the total. Then tell him to remember a card at the same number from the face as his remembered total. In other words, if he has seven cards, he would remember the 7th card you deal.

Deal cards one at a time off the face of the deck into a tabled heap. Stop the deal when you've dealt 14 cards onto the table. Spectator "A" has noted and remembered a card as described above. Pick up the 14-card packet and replace it on the face of the deck.

Ask spectator "B" to count his cards. He too is to note a card in a corresponding position as you deal from the face of the deck. Thus, if he holds five cards, he would remember the 5th card you deal. In fact, you deal 14 cards off the face of the deck, dealing one card at a time onto a heap on the table. When you've dealt 14 cards, turn the deck face-down and replace it in your left hand. Then pick up the tabled packet of 14 cards, turn it face-down and place it on top of the deck.

Take spectator "A's" cards and place them face-down on top of the deck. Then take spectator "B's" cards and place them face-down on the table. Drop the deck on top of "B's" cards and square up the complete deck.

Now spread the pack face-up on the table and run your finger along the cards from top to face until you reach the 15th card from the top. This is spectator "A's" card. Push it out of the deck and ask spectator "A" to verify that this is indeed the card he noted.

When he admits that this is the card, you say, "Actually, anyone could find the cards without even looking at their faces. The reason is that one card will give a stronger impression than the others. It will always stand out."

Turn the pack face-down and spread the deck across the table. The single blue-backed card in the otherwise red-backed deck will stand out like a beacon. Remove the blue-backed card and turn it face-up to reveal that it is indeed spectator "B's" card.

55. IT'S IN THE BAG

A card is chosen and returned to the deck. The deck is then dropped into an empty paper bag. As an afterthought, the magician drops the card case into the bag also. He then twists the mouth of the bag and asks the spectator to shake the bag to give the cards a good mixing.

"You will now see," the performer announces, "a demonstration of fabulous skill, dedication and good looks." He reaches into the bag, claiming that he can instantly find the chosen card. Immediately his hand is withdrawn, and in it is the card case. He acts puzzled for a moment, then opens the case and finds the chosen card INSIDE the card case!

Method: Although easy to do, this trick can have a strong impact on the audience because of the completely unexpected manner in which you find the chosen card. If the deck you are using is blue-backed, note the top card, which we will say is the Eight of Diamonds, and find the duplicate Eight of Diamonds in a deck of matching back design and color. Place the duplicate Eight of Diamonds in your right jacket pocket. Place the deck back into its case with the original Eight of Diamonds still on top.

When you are ready to perform a few card tricks,

remove the deck from the card case, but leave the Eight of Diamonds behind in the card case. Then tuck the flap of the case in so that the card case is closed. Do this in a nonchalant manner, calling no attention to it. When the card case is closed, perform a few tricks with the deck to impress upon the audience that the deck is unprepared and quite ordinary.

To perform "It's in the Bag," proceed as follows. Invite a spectator to shuffle and cut the deck. Then take it back from him and drop it into your right jacket pocket. Position the deck in the pocket so that the duplicate Eight of Diamonds already in the pocket will end up as the face or bottom card of the deck.

Ask a spectator to think of a number from 1 to 20. Then remove cards from the top of your deck and place them face-down onto the table. Count aloud as you do this. When you reach the spectator's number, have him call stop. Then remove the next card—but in fact you remove the Eight of Diamonds from the bottom of the deck—and show him this card. Tell him to remember it.

Replace the Eight of Diamonds in the pocket. Make sure it goes back on the bottom of the deck. Then remove the deck from the pocket, but leave the Eight of Diamonds behind. Assemble the entire deck and drop it into a borrowed paper bag. (If a bag is not readily available, you can use a large handkerchief or a scarf to hold the pack.) Almost as an afterthought, pick up the card case and drop it into the bag, saying, "We might as well get everything in that will fit."

Twist the mouth of the bag and let a spectator shake it to mix the cards. Remark that you will reach into the bag and instantly remove the chosen card. Open the mouth of the bag, reach in and immediately remove the card case. Act puzzled for a moment, saying, "I was certain you picked a thinner card." Then snap your fingers as if remembering where the card might be. Open the flap of the card case and remove the Eight of Diamonds. Say to the assisting spectator, "You shook the bag so hard, you shook the chosen card right into the card case."

REVELATIONS

The card expert who desires to entertain as well as baffle his audience knows that the key to an entertaining card effect lies almost entirely in the novel way a chosen card is revealed. The tricks in this chapter were selected with this end in mind; each is an entertaining and amusing way of revealing a chosen card.

56. THE 3½ OF CLUBS

This trick, a variation of a routine marketed some years ago, is a most unusual way of revealing a chosen card. Prior to the performance, place the Seven of Clubs on top of the deck. This is the major preparation. To present the trick, run through the cards, saying you will remove a prediction card. Slip the prediction card (the Three of Clubs) into the card case for safekeeping.

Then ask the spectator for the first name of anyone close to him. He might say "Jane." Spell J – A – N – E, dealing a card off the top of the deck for each letter. Explain to the spectator that you want him to spell to a card in the same way. Pick up the cards you have just dealt onto the table and replace them on top of the deck.

The spectator takes the deck, spells J – A – N – E, dealing a card off the top for each letter, and looks at the last card he dealt. This card will be the Seven of Clubs, but of course you pretend you do not know the name of the card.

After he has looked at his card, tell him that your

prediction inside the card case will be the same suit as his card and exactly half the value. If he reflects on this for a second, he will realize the impossibility of your claim; since he chose the 7C, your prediction, in order for it to be *exactly* half the value of his card, would have to be the 3½ of Clubs.

Ask him to name his card. He does, and you act a bit taken aback, as if you too realize your predicament. Then say, "As a matter of fact, I did place the Three and a half of Clubs in the card case." Reach into the card case and remove the 3C. Then tip the card case up, allowing a half dollar to slide out. Say, "There it is, the three . . . and a half."

Of course it should be clear that you secretly placed the half dollar in the card case prior to performing the trick.

57. THE GEIGER COUNTER CARD TRICK

This amusing and bewildering card trick perfectly exemplifies how a novel premise can be used to bring about an effect so different that it is certain to be remembered by audiences. Any deck is used.

Explain to the audience that when cards are handled by the audience, the energy level of the cards will increase. You further explain that certain cards, like the Ace of Spades, are sensitive to these energy changes and can detect them in much the same way that a geiger counter detects radiation.

Run through the deck and toss out the Ace of Spades. As you do, have ample opportunity to remember the top card of the deck.

Place the deck face-down on the table. Invite a spectator to cut off about half the deck and invite him to pick up the top half. Then have him remove a card from that half, drop it on top of the packet and cut the packet to lose the chosen card. Then have him drop this half of the deck on top of the other half, and give the complete deck

another cut to further insure that the chosen card is completely lost in the pack.

Take the deck, turn it face-up and spread it on the
table from right to left. Place your left hand on the card at
the extreme left of the spread. Simply rest the hand on
this card to keep it in place. With the right hand take the
Ace of Spades and run it from left to right across the
spread so that the lower index corner slides along the cards
as shown in Figure 25. As the hand moves from left to

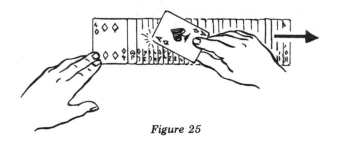

Figure 25

right (in the direction of the arrow), the index corner of
the Ace clicks along from card to card; if done at a moder-
ate speed, the series of clicks that is produced sounds sur-
prisingly like the clicks that are produced by a geiger
counter or scintillation counter.

If the right hand grips the Ace tightly, the clicks are
loud and sharp. If the right hand relaxes its grip, the clicks
become softer. This is the key to the mystery. When you
spread the deck face-up on the table, spot the Locator
Card (the one you glimpsed as being the top card of the
deck). The card just to the right of it is the spectator's
card.

Starting with the Ace of Spades at the far left side of
the spread, hold it loosely in the right hand and run the
card from left to right. When you get near the chosen card,
increase pressure slightly on the Ace of Spades and the
clicks will become noticeably louder. Repeat this action
several times, finally homing in on the area around the Key
Card. Then bring the Ace of Spades to a stop when it is
resting directly on the spectator's chosen card. Name the

chosen card and have the spectator confirm that he did indeed choose this card.

This clever and baffling trick was devised by John Cornelius and is a variation of a trick developed by Jerry Andrus.

58. OPPOSITES ATTRACT

This novel routine uses the four Kings and the four Queens. Explaining that the old saying, "Opposites attract," holds true even with playing cards, the magician has the spectator choose four cards from the packet of eight. When the cards are paired, it is found that the spectator has successfully paired each King with a Queen.

Method: Any deck may be used. Tell the audience that you will use the Kings and Queens. Hold the deck so that only you can see the faces. Run through the cards and remove the four Kings, placing each face-down into a common heap on the table. Then remove the four Queens and place these onto the Kings. You must get across the idea that you are removing Kings and Queens randomly as you come to them. Thus, as you remove each of them, you might say something like, "Here's a Queen, and here's a King . . . here's another King, etc."

UPJOGGED CARDS

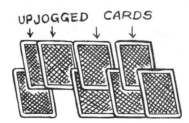

Figure 26

Spread the cards on the table from left to right so they overlap. Then ask the spectator to pull any four cards out of the spread. He should pull each out about halfway. There is no restriction on his choice. He can choose any four cards. The four cards he may decide on are shown as the upjogged cards in Figure 26.

When he has decided on four cards, carefully square the packet, still keeping his cards outjogged. Then strip out the four upjogged cards as a block and place this packet face-down on the table. Pick up the remaining four cards and say, "I want to be sure there are four cards in each group. I don't want to miss any." Count these four cards onto the table, one card on top of the next, thus reversing their order.

You now have two packets on the table, each face-down. Pick up the top card of each group. Comment again about how opposites attract. Then turn these two cards over together to show a King and a Queen. Repeat with each of the next three pairs of cards, and in each case you will find a King paired with a Queen.

59. 60 SECONDS FLAT

A card that is freely chosen by a spectator is returned to the deck, whereupon the chosen card vanishes completely from the deck and penetrates the tabletop. It takes exactly 60 seconds for the chosen card to work its way through the tabletop. At the end of that time, when it has dropped through, it is caught in the middle of the deck in a face-up or reversed condition.

A skeptical spectator may wish to sign the card at the beginning of the routine just to insure that you are not using trick cards, but in fact the deck is ordinary.

Method: Before beginning the trick, secretly reverse the bottom card of the deck. We will assume this card is the Jack of Diamonds. With the deck face-down in the left hand, the bottom card is the face-up Jack of Diamonds. Naturally the audience is unaware of the presence of this reversed card.

Spread the cards from hand to hand and have one chosen. We'll say it is the Ace of Hearts. The card may be signed. Place it face-down on the table. Then place the deck face-down on top of this card. Press down on top of the deck with the right forefinger, saying that this will cause the spectator's card to leave the deck and slowly penetrate the table.

Remarking that it takes exactly 60 seconds for the chosen card to make its way through the tabletop, you add that this is just enough time to show the audience that the card really has vanished from the deck. Pick up the deck and place it into the left hand.

Push off the top ten or twelve cards, turn them face-up and show that the signed Ace of Hearts is not among them. Place this group of cards face-up on the table. Drop the face-down deck on top of these cards.

Pick up the deck and return it to the left hand. Push off another dozen or so cards from the top of the deck and show the Ace of Hearts is not among them either. Place this group face-up on the table. Then drop the face-down deck onto this group.

Repeat the above process of taking cards off the top, showing them and placing them face-up on the bottom of the deck until the Jack of Diamonds shows up. Stop at this point, because the audience will assume that they have seen the face of every card in the deck, and that the signed Ace has truly vanished.

Keeping the deck face-up, cut it and complete the cut. Say to the audience, "Your card should be just about completely through the tabletop. Maybe I can catch it as it falls through."

Place the face-up deck under the table and rap it up against the tabletop. Bring the deck up into view and spread it face-up on the table. There will be one face-down card in the center, and when it is turned over it will be the spectator's signed card.

60. PERSONALITY

Tell the spectator that many people believe in the practice of numerology. It is well known that everyone has a certain unique number associated with his or her character. Then add, "I would say, for instance, that you are an honest, decent person. These qualities are denoted by the numbers 5 and 3. Therefore, if my guess is correct, you are a 5-3 personality."

Hand the spectator a small packet of cards and tell him to place them behind his back. Say, "Let's see if I'm right. Shuffle the cards I've given you. Then turn the top card of the packet face-up, and turn the bottom card of the packet face-up. Shuffle the cards after you've done this."

Repeat the above process as often as the spectator likes. Each time he reverses the top and bottom card, and then gives the packet a shuffle. When he has finished, have him bring out the packet and spread it on the table. Five cards will point one way and three cards the other, exactly as you stated.

Method: This trick was created by Bob Hummer. Before doing it, count off eight cards and place them in your jacket pocket. When they are in the pocket, secretly turn the bottom card of the packet over so it is reversed.

When ready to perform the trick, explain how personality traits are determined by numbers. Tell the spectator that he looks like a 5-3 personality. Then remove the packet from the pocket and hand it to him behind his back.

Have him follow the procedure outlined above for reversing pairs of cards and shuffling the packet. After he has done this several times, he brings the packet out into view and finds that five cards face one way and three the other. On rare occasions you will find *one* card facing one way and *seven* the other; should this happen, simply remark, "I was wrong. You're one of a kind."

61. JUMPING JOKER

This is possibly one of the most dramatic ways of revealing a chosen card. After the card is returned to the center of the deck, the magician snaps the end of the deck. The Joker literally jumps out of the deck, and right next to it is found the chosen card.

There is some slight preparation but it is worth it because of the extremely visual nature of the effect. Remove the Joker from the deck and tear off the lower right quarter as shown in Figure 27. Discard the lower quarter, as it is not needed. Now turn the Joker over side-for-side and drop the deck on top of it. The Joker thus becomes the bottom card of the face-down deck, and the missing corner is at the lower left.

Spread the deck and have a card chosen. Tell the spectator to replace it on top of the deck. Then cut the deck at about the middle and complete the cut to lose the chosen card.

Thus far all is fair. Tell the audience that through years of dedication, self-denial, etc., you've managed to teach the Joker to find cards for you. All you have to do, in fact, is riffle the deck and the Joker will pop up immediately at the right location.

As you talk, bevel the deck slightly so it looks like Figure 28. Then grasp it at the lower left corner by the left thumb on top, first finger below.

The right fingers now riffle the outer or upper right corner of the deck, the portion marked "X" in Figure 28. The riffle is begun at the face of the face-down deck and works toward the back. The riffle is done quickly, with a snap of the fingers. A few minutes' practice will be enough to acquire the knack of doing this.

Figure 27

Figure 28

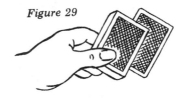

Figure 29

Odd as it may seem on reading this, the Joker will indeed pop up out of the center of the pack, as shown in Figure 29. If you have never seen it before, it is a startling sight.

When the Joker has popped up into view, lower the deck so the backs of the cards are visible to the audience. The right hand then lifts up the Joker plus the cards above it and places these momentarily in the right jacket pocket. The right hand then turns over the top card of the deck and it is the chosen card.

The reason for placing the top half plus the Joker into the pocket is that you want to unload the Joker before the audience gets a chance to examine it. Leave the Joker in the pocket as you bring out the rest of the packet from the pocket. Shuffle this packet into the balance of the deck. If someone wants to examine the deck at this point, just make sure you have a regular Joker in the deck for them to find.

The idea of causing a torn-corner card to pop up out of the deck as described above is not new, but its use in the location of a chosen card is novel and sure to make an impact on the audience.

62. CALCULATOR CARDS

This is a comedy effect suggested by Richard Himber in which a spectator's card is "calculated" to be exactly six and three quarters from the top of the deck. Oddly enough, the calculation does prove to be exact.

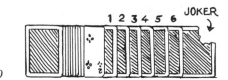

Figure 30

Preparation is easy. Take a Joker and tear out a quarter of it. You can use the same Joker that was used in the "Jumping Joker" effect. The torn Joker is placed on the bottom of the deck. Above it are six more cards, then the face-up Two of Clubs, then the balance of the deck. The complete set-up is shown in Figure 30.

When ready to present the trick, have a spectator choose a card from the middle of the deck. Square the deck and have the chosen card replaced on top, then cut the deck and complete the cut.

State that you use a certain Calculator Card that is absolutely infallible. Run the cards from hand to hand until you come to the face-up Two of Clubs. Cut the Two of Clubs to the top of the deck. Then place the deuce face-up on the table.

Say, "It's all quite simple. Taking the value of the Two of Clubs, its relative location in the deck, the time of day and the logarithm of my license plate number, we arrive at a magic number, in this case—mmmm, exactly six and three quarters."

With a self-satisfied look, you conclude, "In other words, your card is exactly six and three quarters down in the deck. Amazing, isn't it?" The spectator, having never heard of a card being six and three quarters down in the deck, will be less than impressed, let alone amazed.

Slowly and dramatically you deal cards off the top, calling out, "1 . . . 2 . . ." and so on, until you arrive at the card just before the torn Joker, which you count as 6. After dealing this card, deal the Joker, saying, "And three quarters, making a total of six and three quarters." While the audience laughs at the gag, turn over the next card and show it is the chosen card.

63. PROCESS OF ELIMINATION

A novel and offbeat way of revealing a previously chosen card, this is based on what is known as the "plunger principle," credited to Jack McMillan.

A small amount of preparation is required. Arrange the 2S – 3S – 4S – 5S on top of the deck in that order, the 2S being the top card. With this done beforehand, you are now ready to present the trick. Spread the pack face-down between the hands and invite a spectator to choose a card from the middle. He can take any card except the top four cards of the deck.

When he chooses a card, square up the deck and place it on the table face-down. Have him drop his chosen card on top of the deck. Then have him cut the deck and complete the cut. Take the deck from him, turn it face-up so that you can see the faces, and run through the pack until you come to the 5S. You then upjog every other card beginning at the 5S and working back toward the top of the deck until you have five cards upjogged. Figure 31 shows the first four cards being upjogged. You will upjog one more at the left according to the above procedure.

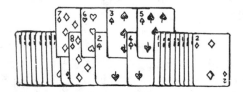

Figure 31

Call attention to the fact that the face card of the upjogged packet is the Five of Spades. Then say, "We'll find your card by a process of elimination."

Place the right forefinger on top of the upjogged packet and push down as indicated in Figure 32. Because of the plunger action of the interlaced cards, the upper packet slides in flush with the deck; at the same time another packet will be forced out the bottom of the deck, as in Figure 33. As soon as it appears, say, "We've eliminated the Five and now we have a Four." Now push up on the lower packet so that it slides in flush with the deck. The result of this action is to force a smaller packet out from the top of the deck with a Three showing.

Push this packet down flush with the deck. A still smaller packet will be forced down and out of the bottom of the pack with a Two showing. Finally push this small packet up so it is flush with the deck. This time a single card will slide up and out of the top of the pack and it will be the card chosen by the spectator.

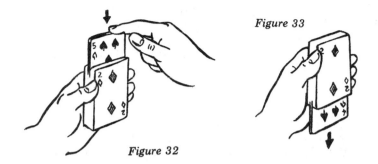

Figure 33

Figure 32

A few notes on the handling. In order for this trick to work smoothly the cards cannot be sticky or overly worn. If you find that the trick does not work the first few times you try it, chances are that you are not exerting enough pressure on the deck with the left hand. This is not to imply that the trick is difficult or unreliable in working. Once you acquaint yourself with the basic principle you'll find that the trick works easily and infallibly.

64. THE JOKER KNOWS

In this subtle routine, the creation of Theodore Annemann, the magician uses the All-Knowing, All-Seeing, etc., Joker to find the selected card. The omnipotent Joker does not do as well as advertised, and after repeatedly failing to find the chosen card, it changes into the chosen card itself. The fact that this happens with the Joker in the spectator's hands when the change occurs adds much to the mystery.

Without the knowledge of the audience, you start with the Joker on the bottom of the pack. Spread the cards and have one chosen. Square up the deck, and place it on the table. Have the spectator drop his card on top, and then cut the deck to lose his card somewhere in the middle.

Take the deck and announce that you will use the All-Knowing, All-Seeing, And Other Favorable Qualities

Too Numerous To Mention, Joker. Turn the deck face-up and look over the faces of the cards until you spot the Joker. However, you do not remove the Joker from the deck. Instead, you remove the card directly below it. Without revealing the face of this card to the audience but implying it is the Joker, place it face-down on the table (it is the chosen card).

Place the deck face-up on the table. Ask a spectator to insert the face-down "Joker" (really the chosen card) into the face-up pack at any point. When he's done this, spread the deck face-up on the table. Point to the face-down card and announce, "The Joker has infallibly found your card. It is of course the card directly above the Infallible Joker." The spectator will tell you that the card above the supposed Joker is not his.

"Of course I meant the card immediately *below* the Infallible Joker." No, the spectator says, that is not it either. Act disappointed and say, "When I think of how much I paid for this Joker. . . ." You then remember something. "Just out of curiosity, what card did you choose?" The spectator might say the Eight of Spades. You reply, "Yes, that was the *one* card the Joker couldn't find. When someone picks the Eight of Spades, here's what happens." Remove the face-down card (the supposed Joker) from the deck and snap your fingers over it. Then have the spectator turn it over to reveal that it has changed to his chosen card, the Eight of Spades.

65. THE CONTROLLED CUT

Here you teach a spectator how to cut the deck in such a way that he has complete control over the cards. If, for example, he cuts to a 7-spot, a previously chosen card is found exactly 7 down from the top of the deck.

Secretly remove all 13 Hearts from the deck. Arrange them in order from Ace to King, with the Ace at the face or bottom of the packet and the King on top. Place the packet face-down on the table and then drop the face-down deck on top of the packet. Case the deck until you plan to perform this trick.

To present the routine, remove the deck from its case and then spread the cards and have one chosen from the middle. Square up the deck and place it on the table. Instruct the spectator to drop his card on top and then cut the deck to lose the chosen card.

It is at this point that a bit of acting comes into play. Pretend to notice something about the way he cut the deck. Have him cut the deck again and complete the cut. Ask him to do it once more, then once again and complete the cut. Ask him to do it once more, then once again. Each time you appear to notice something of particular interest about the way he cuts the deck. Remark that he has a light touch with the cards, exactly what is needed in controlled cuts.

Turn the deck face-up and have him cut the deck and complete the cut. Congratulate him, but add that he should use a lighter touch. Have him cut the deck again, and continue the process of encouragement. He cuts the deck again and again until a Heart shows up at the face of the deck. Stop him at this point and tell him he has done remarkably well. If the face card is the Seven of Hearts, call attention to its value. Then turn the deck face-down. Have the spectator deal off seven cards. The last card he deals will be his chosen card.

By way of a reference, I do not know the exact source of the principle used here, but believe Al Baker should be credited with the basic premise.

MIRACLES WITH CARDS

If you have studied and mastered the tricks in the preceding pages, and have had an opportunity to try them out on friends, then you will have developed a certain self-confidence in the presentation of card effects. This means that you will be ready to tackle the tricks in this final chapter; they require a bit more study, a bit more attention to detail, but the end result should be worth it; in all cases, if properly presented, these card routines seem to lie beyond rational explanation.

Some, like "Quick as a Wink" (No. 72) and "Topsy-Turvy" (No. 71), are visually startling. Others, like the "O. Henry Card Trick" (No. 69; a favorite of J. W. Sarles), pack a double climax that the audience will not quickly forget. They are not meant to be presented one after another. Rather, you should intersperse these stronger routines with quick tricks like Locations and Poker Deals.

66. FOLLOW THE LEADER

This classic effect dates back to the time of Robert-Houdin. There are many elaborate ways of bringing about the basic trick, some of them requiring sophisticated sleight-of-hand ability. The following is a simple method that achieves the desired end without sleight-of-hand. It is a variation of a method suggested by J. W. Sarles.

Invite a spectator to remove three red cards and three black cards from the deck. When he has done this, instruct him to arrange the cards so the colors alternate red-black-red-black-red-black from the top down. It is important to let the spectator alternate the colors so he is certain there has been no hanky-panky at this stage of the trick.

Take the packet from him and hold it face-up in the left hand. As you say "Remember that the colors alternate," take the first card into the right hand. This is the face card of the face-up packet. As you take it, say "Black." Then take the next card on top of it. Say "Red" as you take it. Then place this pair of cards in back of the packet.

For the second pair the handling is slightly different. Push the face card to the right and say "Black." Then push the next card to the right and say "Red." Take this pair of cards with the right hand and place them behind the packet. Note that here you do *not* reverse the order of the two cards as they are taken into the right hand.

For the third and final pair of cards, take the first one into the right hand and say "Black." Then take the next card on top of it and say "Red." Place this pair of cards in back of the packet.

Turn the packet face-down and replace it in the left hand. Now deal from left to right, dealing the cards into two heaps, alternating the deal so the first card goes into the left heap, the next into the right heap, the next into the left heap, etc. As you deal, say, "Black, red, black, red, black, red," making it clear to the audience that all the blacks are in the left heap, all the reds in the right heap.

Turn up the top card of each heap and place it above its own heap. Call these "Leader Cards." As shown in Figure 34, the black Leader Card may be the Five of Spades. The red Leader Card will be the Six of Hearts.

Say, "The black cards are all on the left and the red cards are on the right. Let's exchange the Leader Cards." Pick up the 5S and the 6H, exchange them, and place the 5S still face-up but in front of the right packet. Place the face-up 6H in front of the left packet.

"If we exchange the Leader Cards like that, the colors will follow the leaders." Pick up the top card of each

Figure 34

face-down packet. Do not exchange them. Simply rub or touch the face-down card in the left hand on the red Leader Card and turn it face-up to show it has become red. Then touch the card in the right hand to the 5S, turn it over and show that this card has suddenly become black. The situation at this point is shown in Figure 35.

Place these face-up cards on top of their respective Leader Cards; in Figure 35 you would place the 4D face-up onto the 6H and the 2C face-up onto the 5S.

Figure 35

Then say, "We can exchange the other cards and it will still work." Now openly exchange the two face-down cards. Pick up the one on the left, snap it face-up and show that it has changed into a red card. Then turn over the one at the right and show it has suddenly changed to a black card.

67. MENTAL MIRACLE

To perform this seemingly miraculous feat, no special preparation or dexterity is called for. You can use any borrowed deck, and the trick is performed as soon as the deck is made available. While you turn your back, the spectator sitting across from you shuffles and cuts the deck. He then hands the deck under the table to you. From this point on, the deck is kept out of sight under the table. The mentalist (that is, you) spreads the deck and has the spectator select any card. The spectator returns this card anywhere in the deck and immediately takes the deck and shuffles it.

No one knows where the chosen card is, and from this point on the mentalist never touches the deck again. When the spectator is satisfied that the deck is well shuffled, he deals cards off the top one at a time and hands them under the table to the mentalist. As each card is taken, the mentalist concentrates for a moment, then shakes his head and says, "No, this isn't it." Each card is then placed face-down onto the table.

At some point the mentalist will be handed the card chosen by the spectator. When he gets it, he concentrates as before, then he says, "Yes, I think this is it. A black card, wasn't it? The Four of Spades?"

Remember that the deck is borrowed, and is shuffled and cut by the spectator before and after he chooses a card. Also, once the chosen card is returned to the deck, the spectator keeps the deck, and he may shuffle it at *any* time thereafter. This feat is strong enough to fool even well-versed magicians. Properly built up, it can become a feature mental effect for anyone who knows the secret.

Method: As is the case with many of the most impressive tricks, this one rests on a simple premise. After the deck is shuffled and handed to you under the table, invite a spectator to remove any card. After he does, simply turn the deck over. This is done secretly, and since the deck is under the table, no one is aware of what you did.

The selected card is returned to the deck. Naturally the spectator, after looking at his card, returns it face-down into the deck, thinking that the deck itself is face-down. But in fact he is returning the card face-down to a face-up deck, so his card is automatically reversed in the pack. Once his card has been returned, turn the deck over so it is face-down, and immediately hand it under the table to the spectator for shuffling.

When he is satisfied that the deck is well mixed, ask him to give you cards one at a time off the top. The deck remains under the table. The spectator hands you the first card. Take it, pretend to concentrate, then shake your head and bring the card up and toss it onto the table. The card is face-down when the spectator gives it to you, and remains face-down when you bring it up from under the table.

But there will come a point where the card handed to you by the spectator is face-up. You will know this as soon as you *begin* to bring the card up from under the table, but *before* the card can be seen by the spectator. A very slight downward glance will allow you to see the face of this card. Place it back under the table as you say, "Wait a minute. I think this may be it. You chose a black card, didn't you?" Then go on to name the card. Turn it face-down, bring it up from under the table and slowly turn it over to reveal it to be the chosen card.

The basic premise of this effect was devised by Joseph Dunninger, the eminent mentalist. The method is the author's variation of an idea suggested by Clayton Rawson.

68. TWINS

Two decks are used. Each deck is shuffled by the spectator and each deck is placed in a handkerchief. Taking a Joker in each hand, the magician slides each Joker under the handkerchief containing a deck. When the first Joker is removed, it has changed to the Four of Spades.

When the second Joker is removed from under the other handkerchief, it too has changed to the Four of Spades!

Method: You will need one red-backed deck and one blue-backed deck. Each deck must contain a Joker at the beginning. That is the only preparation, an easy matter to arrange even if using borrowed decks.

Explain to the audience that you will use just the two Jokers. Run through the blue-backed deck and remove the Joker. Let the audience plainly see the face of the Joker, then turn the Joker face-down and place it on the table. Hand the blue-backed deck to a spectator for shuffling.

Take back the blue-backed deck after it is well mixed and wrap it in a handkerchief. The handkerchief should be cotton or linen, preferably white, because as you wrap up the deck it is necessary to glimpse the bottom card of the deck through the handkerchief. Generally, a white handkerchief is translucent enough to allow you to glimpse the bottom card through a thickness of the cloth (this method of glimpsing a card was suggested by Nate Leipsig). We'll say the glimpsed card is the Four of Spades.

Now say that you will remove the Joker from the red-backed deck. Run through this deck and pretend to remove the Joker. But in fact remove the Four of Spades and place it face-down on the table without the audience seeing the face of the card. Immediately hand the red-backed deck out for shuffling. Then have the spectator wrap it loosely in a second handkerchief.

Pick up the blue-backed Joker in one hand and the supposed red-backed Joker in the other. Say to the audience that you will slip each card back into its own deck momentarily. Remind the audience that the decks were shuffled and cut *after* you removed the Jokers, so you could not possibly know a single card in either deck.

Slip the blue-backed Joker under the handkerchief around the blue-backed deck and slide the Joker into that pack. Remove the face card of the blue-backed deck (the Four of Spades in our example) and bring this card out from under the handkerchief in a face-down condition.

Then place the red-backed card—the supposed other Joker—under the handkerchief wrapped around the red-backed deck. Pause for a moment, then remove this same card.

Turn over the blue-backed card and show that the Joker has changed to the Four of Spades. Then turn over the red-backed card and show that it too has changed to the Four of Spades.

69. O. HENRY CARD TRICK

One of the strongest types of card magic you can do is the trick which has a double ending. Thus, you perform a trick and bring it to a successful conclusion. Just when the audience thinks the trick is over, you then reveal a further climax even more startling than the original. The following is an example of the genre: you start out by performing a prediction trick, but then the trick takes a strange turn.

Required are 20 black cards and a single red card. We will say the red card is the Queen of Hearts. Place this card 10th from the top of the packet of black cards.

Place the packet on the table in a face-down condition. While you turn your back, ask a spectator to remove a small packet of cards from the top. He can remove from one to ten cards. Tell him to secretly count the cards and hide them in his jacket pocket.

Pretend to concentrate for a moment. Then jot down a prediction on a slip of paper. The prediction reads, "You will choose the Queen of Hearts." Fold the prediction slip in half and in half again. Give it to a spectator to hold, specifying that they hold it at their fingertips so the prediction is in view at all times.

Now pick up the balance of the packet on the table. Deal cards singly off the top into a face-down row on the table, dealing *from right to left*, until you have dealt a total of ten cards.

Ask the spectator how many cards he hid in his

pocket, explaining that whatever the number, you will use this number to locate a card in a fair and random manner. Let us say he placed six cards in his pocket. Instruct him to count to the sixth card, beginning at the left end of the row and counting *from left to right*. When he's done this, he turns up the next card to the right. In our example it will be the Queen of Hearts.

The spectator entrusted with the prediction now opens the prediction slip and reads aloud that you correctly predicted the Queen of Hearts would be chosen.

The trick appears to be over. Have the spectator add his pocketed cards to those on the table. All cards are face-down at this point except the Queen of Hearts, but you pretend to notice something. Pause for a moment as if studying the cards. Then say, "That's odd. Not only did you pick the card I predicted, but you picked the only red card in the entire packet." As you say this, turn up bunches of cards until the entire packet is face-up and spread out on the table, revealing that every card is black except the chosen card.

The key to success in tricks of this type (as in all card magic) is the ability to act convincingly. You must give the impression that the entire point of the trick is a prediction. The second climax, where it is discovered that the spectator chose the only red card in a large packet of blacks, then comes as a baffling finish.

70. ASTRO TWINS

In this amusing and puzzling trick, cards are chosen by two spectators and the chosen cards placed face-down on the table, side by side. Now the spectators change places. When the cards are turned up it is seen that they have acted in sympathy and they too have changed places.

Method: For maximum dramatic impact, you should have the two spectators seated directly across the table from you. We'll say spectator "A" is the spectator to your left and spectator "B" is the spectator to your right.

Tell them you will use a small batch of cards. You apparently take a haphazard number of cards off the top of the deck but in fact take exactly 20 cards.

Hand the packet to spectator "A." Ask him to fan the cards so he can see the faces. Then have him note a card and its position from the top. Thus he might note the Five of Diamonds, which might be 10th from the top.

He squares the packet and hands it to spectator "B." This spectator then fans the cards and also notes a card and its position. He might note the Queen of Spades, 12th from the top.

Take back the packet from spectator "B." When you get the packet, say to the audience, "Let's see how many cards we have." Deal cards off the top of the packet into a heap on the table. Continue the deal until all cards have been dealt. Then, saying, "We have exactly 20 cards," replace the packet in the left hand and casually transfer the top card to the bottom of the packet.

Ask each party for his number (position from the top). Add them together. The total will be either more or less than 20 (and on rare occasions exactly 20). If the total is more than 20, say, "We'll need that many more cards to bring up our total." In our case the total of the two numbers will be 10 plus 12, or 22. Thus, to bring the total up to 22, you must deal two cards off the top of the deck onto the packet. Now the packet contains 22 cards.

(If the total is less than 20, say, "In this case we won't need all these cards." Remove as many cards as necessary to make the number of cards in the packet equal to the total of the spectators' numbers. To take an example, suppose spectator "A's" card was 5th from the top and "B's" card was 9th. The total of these two numbers is 14. Thus, you would remove six cards from the top of the 20-card packet and discard them. This reduces the packet so it now contains exactly 14 cards.)

Remind the audience that you have no idea which card was chosen by whom. All you know is the location of each card. Count down in the packet to the number named by spectator "A" and place the card at that position face-down in front of him. Continue the count until you reach the other spectator's number and place the card at that number in front of him.

"All we've done so far," you say, "is give each of you your card back. But let me show you something odd. Would you get out of your chairs and change places?" Spectators "A" and "B" change places. For the unexpected finish you show that the chosen cards have acted in sympathy and have also changed places; instead of "A's" card being in front of spectator "B" and vice-versa, "A's" card is in front of "A" once again, and "B's" card is in front of "B!"

A note might be appropriate regarding those few cases where "A's" number, when added to "B's" number, totals exactly 20. In these instances you do not add cards to your packet nor remove cards from the packet. Simply use the 20-card packet as is.

Also, in the above example you counted down to "A's" card first. This is because "A's" number was smaller than "B's." In all cases you count first to the smaller of the two numbers and place that card before the appropriate spectator. Then continue the count to the larger of the two numbers and place the card at that number before the other spectator. The rest of the trick is as written.

71. TOPSY-TURVY

Here the spectator brings about the magical reversal of two chosen cards with the deck in his own hands. The deck may be borrowed, as it is unprepared. The trick itself requires no skill.

Take the deck and spread it face-up on the table. Tell the spectator that you could have him pick a card with the deck face-up, but that you would rather have his choice be a completely random one. As you talk, note the card that lies second from the bottom or face of the deck. In Figure 36 this card is the 5S.

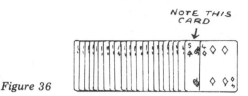

Figure 36

Square up the deck and turn it face-down. Invite the spectator to lift off about half the deck and place his cards behind his back. You then take the remainder of the deck (the bottom half) and place it behind your back.

Instruct the spectator to select a card at random from his half of the deck. You pretend to do likewise, but what you really do is to remove the bottom card, turn it over and replace it on the bottom of the packet. Then turn the second card from the bottom over in place. Finally, turn the entire packet over. The end result is shown in Figure 37. The previously noted card, the 5S in our example, is now the second card from the top of your packet.

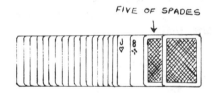

Figure 37

You and the spectator bring your respective packets out in front. Tell him to look at the card he randomly chose. Then take his card and insert it face-down into the center of your packet. Remove the top card of your packet, pretend to look at it, and have the spectator bury it in the middle of his half of the deck.

When this has been done, tell him that he might be able to find his own card by a random process known as Transverse Deflection (this is gibberish, but it sounds impressive). Hand him your half behind his back. As your packet is placed behind his back, turn the packet over before he takes it. Then tell him to hold the packet at right angles to the floor and to give it a sudden sharp twist so it is parallel to the floor.

Take the packet back from him. Spread the cards and show that the sudden sharp movement caused his card to turn face up in the deck. Remove his card and drop it onto the table. Then drop your packet (still face-down) onto his packet and square the deck. Hand him the entire deck behind his back and ask if he might try by the same process to find your card (here you simply name the card you glimpsed at the beginning of the trick), the Five of Spades.

When he has gone through the Transverse Deflection business, have him bring the deck into view and to spread the cards between his hands. He does and finds the Five of Spades has mysteriously turned face-up in the deck.

72. QUICK AS A WINK

This brilliant trick was originated by Reinhard Muller. The effect is direct and quite startling: a chosen card, hopelessly lost in the deck, suddenly appears between two Aces. The following handling is in part based on an approach described by Harvey Rosenthal.

Before the trick begins, secretly remove the two black Aces from the deck, turn them face-up and place them under the top card of the deck. The set-up thus looks like Figure 38.

Figure 38

Place the deck on the table. Ask a spectator to cut off about half and to place the cut portion (the top half of the deck) off to one side for the moment.

Have him pick up the bottom half of the deck, shuffle it and note a card. Then direct him to place his card on top of the top half of the deck. Finally, he is to give his packet of cards one more shuffle and then drop this packet on top of the chosen card. After he has done this, tell him to carefully square the deck.

Tell him that before the trick commenced, you reversed the black Aces in the pack. As you talk, run the cards from hand to hand until you come to the reversed Aces. Cut the pack at this point and complete the cut so the Aces are the top cards of the pack (the spectator's chosen card is second from the bottom at this point).

Deal the two black Aces onto the table. Remark that these two cards will help you find the spectator's card. Then add, "I hope your card isn't on the top or bottom." When you say this, remove the bottom card, show it and place it in the center of the deck. Then remove the top card, show it and place it into the center of the pack. The spectator will agree that neither of these cards is his.

Now place the Ace of Clubs on top of the pack. Then grasp the deck from above with the right hand. The left hand places the Ace of Spades on the bottom of the pack, but this Ace is jogged or positioned to the left as indicated in Figure 39. The left hand now grasps the deck again as indicated in Figure 40. Note that both Aces are visible to the audience at this point.

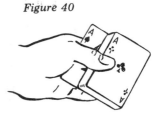

Figure 40

Figure 39

The grip of the left hand is important. Note in Figure 41 that the left first finger rests on the Ace of Spades, whereas the left middle finger rests on the bottom card of the deck. This bottom card, the 5H in Figure 41, is the spectator's chosen card. The left thumb, of course, rests securely on the top card of the deck, the Ace of Clubs.

The left hand now throws the deck into the right, using a sharp throwing motion. The left thumb holds back the Ace of Clubs, while the fingers beneath the deck hold back the Ace of Spades and the spectator's card. The deck is caught by the right hand.

Figure 41   *Figure 42*

The result of the above action leaves the two black Aces in the left hand with the chosen card between them, as in Figure 42. Try it a few times and you will find it a startling visual effect.

A CATALOG OF SELECTED
DOVER BOOKS
IN ALL FIELDS OF INTEREST

A CATALOG OF SELECTED DOVER
BOOKS IN ALL FIELDS OF INTEREST

DRAWINGS OF REMBRANDT, edited by Seymour Slive. Updated Lippmann, Hofstede de Groot edition, with definitive scholarly apparatus. All portraits, biblical sketches, landscapes, nudes. Oriental figures, classical studies, together with selection of work by followers. 550 illustrations. Total of 630pp. 9⅛ × 12¼.
21485-0, 21486-9 Pa., Two-vol. set $25.00

GHOST AND HORROR STORIES OF AMBROSE BIERCE, Ambrose Bierce. 24 tales vividly imagined, strangely prophetic, and decades ahead of their time in technical skill: "The Damned Thing," "An Inhabitant of Carcosa," "The Eyes of the Panther," "Moxon's Master," and 20 more. 199pp. 5⅜ × 8½. 20767-6 Pa. $3.95

ETHICAL WRITINGS OF MAIMONIDES, Maimonides. Most significant ethical works of great medieval sage, newly translated for utmost precision, readability. Laws Concerning Character Traits, Eight Chapters, more. 192pp. 5⅜ × 8½.
24522-5 Pa. $4.50

THE EXPLORATION OF THE COLORADO RIVER AND ITS CANYONS, J. W. Powell. Full text of Powell's 1,000-mile expedition down the fabled Colorado in 1869. Superb account of terrain, geology, vegetation, Indians, famine, mutiny, treacherous rapids, mighty canyons, during exploration of last unknown part of continental U.S. 400pp. 5⅜ × 8½. 20094-9 Pa. $6.95

HISTORY OF PHILOSOPHY, Julián Marías. Clearest one-volume history on the market. Every major philosopher and dozens of others, to Existentialism and later. 505pp. 5⅜ × 8½. 21739-6 Pa. $9.95

ALL ABOUT LIGHTNING, Martin A. Uman. Highly readable non-technical survey of nature and causes of lightning, thunderstorms, ball lightning, St. Elmo's Fire, much more. Illustrated. 192pp. 5⅜ × 8½. 25237-X Pa. $5.95

SAILING ALONE AROUND THE WORLD, Captain Joshua Slocum. First man to sail around the world, alone, in small boat. One of great feats of seamanship told in delightful manner. 67 illustrations. 294pp. 5⅜ × 8½. 20326-3 Pa. $4.95

LETTERS AND NOTES ON THE MANNERS, CUSTOMS AND CONDITIONS OF THE NORTH AMERICAN INDIANS, George Catlin. Classic account of life among Plains Indians: ceremonies, hunt, warfare, etc. 312 plates. 572pp. of text. 6⅛ × 9¼. 22118-0, 22119-9 Pa. Two-vol. set $15.90

ALASKA: The Harriman Expedition, 1899, John Burroughs, John Muir, et al. Informative, engrossing accounts of two-month, 9,000-mile expedition. Native peoples, wildlife, forests, geography, salmon industry, glaciers, more. Profusely illustrated. 240 black-and-white line drawings. 124 black-and-white photographs. 3 maps. Index. 576pp. 5⅜ × 8½. 25109-8 Pa. $11.95

THE BOOK OF BEASTS: Being a Translation from a Latin Bestiary of the Twelfth Century, T. H. White. Wonderful catalog real and fanciful beasts: manticore, griffin, phoenix, amphivius, jaculus, many more. White's witty erudite commentary on scientific, historical aspects. Fascinating glimpse of medieval mind. Illustrated. 296pp. 5⅜ × 8¼. (Available in U.S. only) 24609-4 Pa. $5.95

FRANK LLOYD WRIGHT: ARCHITECTURE AND NATURE With 160 Illustrations, Donald Hoffmann. Profusely illustrated study of influence of nature—especially prairie—on Wright's designs for Fallingwater, Robie House, Guggenheim Museum, other masterpieces. 96pp. 9¼ × 10¾. 25098-9 Pa. $7.95

FRANK LLOYD WRIGHT'S FALLINGWATER, Donald Hoffmann. Wright's famous waterfall house: planning and construction of organic idea. History of site, owners, Wright's personal involvement. Photographs of various stages of building. Preface by Edgar Kaufmann, Jr. 100 illustrations. 112pp. 9¼ × 10. 23671-4 Pa. $7.95

YEARS WITH FRANK LLOYD WRIGHT: Apprentice to Genius, Edgar Tafel. Insightful memoir by a former apprentice presents a revealing portrait of Wright the man, the inspired teacher, the greatest American architect. 372 black-and-white illustrations. Preface. Index. vi + 228pp. 8¼ × 11. 24801-1 Pa. $9.95

THE STORY OF KING ARTHUR AND HIS KNIGHTS, Howard Pyle. Enchanting version of King Arthur fable has delighted generations with imaginative narratives of exciting adventures and unforgettable illustrations by the author. 41 illustrations. xviii + 313pp. 6⅛ × 9¼. 21445-1 Pa. $6.50

THE GODS OF THE EGYPTIANS, E. A. Wallis Budge. Thorough coverage of numerous gods of ancient Egypt by foremost Egyptologist. Information on evolution of cults, rites and gods; the cult of Osiris; the Book of the Dead and its rites; the sacred animals and birds; Heaven and Hell; and more. 956pp. 6⅛ × 9¼. 22055-9, 22056-7 Pa., Two-vol. set $21.90

A THEOLOGICO-POLITICAL TREATISE, Benedict Spinoza. Also contains unfinished *Political Treatise*. Great classic on religious liberty, theory of government on common consent. R. Elwes translation. Total of 421pp. 5⅜ × 8½. 20249-6 Pa. $6.95

INCIDENTS OF TRAVEL IN CENTRAL AMERICA, CHIAPAS, AND YUCATAN, John L. Stephens. Almost single-handed discovery of Maya culture; exploration of ruined cities, monuments, temples; customs of Indians. 115 drawings. 892pp. 5⅜ × 8½. 22404-X, 22405-8 Pa., Two-vol. set $15.90

LOS CAPRICHOS, Francisco Goya. 80 plates of wild, grotesque monsters and caricatures. Prado manuscript included. 183pp. 6⅛ × 9⅜. 22384-1 Pa. $4.95

AUTOBIOGRAPHY: The Story of My Experiments with Truth, Mohandas K. Gandhi. Not hagiography, but Gandhi in his own words. Boyhood, legal studies, purification, the growth of the Satyagraha (nonviolent protest) movement. Critical, inspiring work of the man who freed India. 480pp. 5⅜ × 8½. (Available in U.S. only) 24593-4 Pa. $6.95

ILLUSTRATED DICTIONARY OF HISTORIC ARCHITECTURE, edited by Cyril M. Harris. Extraordinary compendium of clear, concise definitions for over 5,000 important architectural terms complemented by over 2,000 line drawings. Covers full spectrum of architecture from ancient ruins to 20th-century Modernism. Preface. 592pp. 7½ × 9⅜. 24444-X Pa. $15.95

THE NIGHT BEFORE CHRISTMAS, Clement Moore. Full text, and woodcuts from original 1848 book. Also critical, historical material. 19 illustrations. 40pp. 4⅝ × 6. 22797-9 Pa. $2.50

THE LESSON OF JAPANESE ARCHITECTURE: 165 Photographs, Jiro Harada. Memorable gallery of 165 photographs taken in the 1930's of exquisite Japanese homes of the well-to-do and historic buildings. 13 line diagrams. 192pp. 8⅜ × 11¼. 24778-3 Pa. $8.95

THE AUTOBIOGRAPHY OF CHARLES DARWIN AND SELECTED LETTERS, edited by Francis Darwin. The fascinating life of eccentric genius composed of an intimate memoir by Darwin (intended for his children); commentary by his son, Francis; hundreds of fragments from notebooks, journals, papers; and letters to and from Lyell, Hooker, Huxley, Wallace and Henslow. xi + 365pp. 5⅜ × 8. 20479-0 Pa. $6.95

WONDERS OF THE SKY: Observing Rainbows, Comets, Eclipses, the Stars and Other Phenomena, Fred Schaaf. Charming, easy-to-read poetic guide to all manner of celestial events visible to the naked eye. Mock suns, glories, Belt of Venus, more. Illustrated. 299pp. 5¼ × 8¼. 24402-4 Pa. $7.95

BURNHAM'S CELESTIAL HANDBOOK, Robert Burnham, Jr. Thorough guide to the stars beyond our solar system. Exhaustive treatment. Alphabetical by constellation: Andromeda to Cetus in Vol. 1; Chamaeleon to Orion in Vol. 2; and Pavo to Vulpecula in Vol. 3. Hundreds of illustrations. Index in Vol. 3. 2,000pp. 6⅛ × 9¼. 23567-X, 23568-8, 23673-0 Pa., Three-vol. set $38.85

STAR NAMES: Their Lore and Meaning, Richard Hinckley Allen. Fascinating history of names various cultures have given to constellations and literary and folkloristic uses that have been made of stars. Indexes to subjects. Arabic and Greek names. Biblical references. Bibliography. 563pp. 5⅜ × 8½. 21079-0 Pa. $7.95

THIRTY YEARS THAT SHOOK PHYSICS: The Story of Quantum Theory, George Gamow. Lucid, accessible introduction to influential theory of energy and matter. Careful explanations of Dirac's anti-particles, Bohr's model of the atom, much more. 12 plates. Numerous drawings. 240pp. 5⅜ × 8½. 24895-X Pa. $5.95

CHINESE DOMESTIC FURNITURE IN PHOTOGRAPHS AND MEASURED DRAWINGS, Gustav Ecke. A rare volume, now affordably priced for antique collectors, furniture buffs and art historians. Detailed review of styles ranging from early Shang to late Ming. Unabridged republication. 161 black-and-white drawings, photos. Total of 224pp. 8⅜ × 11¼. (Available in U.S. only) 25171-3 Pa. $12.95

VINCENT VAN GOGH: A Biography, Julius Meier-Graefe. Dynamic, penetrating study of artist's life, relationship with brother, Theo, painting techniques, travels, more. Readable, engrossing. 160pp. 5⅜ × 8½. (Available in U.S. only) 25253-1 Pa. $3.95

HOW TO WRITE, Gertrude Stein. Gertrude Stein claimed anyone could understand her unconventional writing—here are clues to help. Fascinating improvisations, language experiments, explanations illuminate Stein's craft and the art of writing. Total of 414pp. 4⅜ × 6⅜. 23144-5 Pa. $5.95

ADVENTURES AT SEA IN THE GREAT AGE OF SAIL: Five Firsthand Narratives, edited by Elliot Snow. Rare true accounts of exploration, whaling, shipwreck, fierce natives, trade, shipboard life, more. 33 illustrations. Introduction. 353pp. 5⅜ × 8½. 25177-2 Pa. $7.95

THE HERBAL OR GENERAL HISTORY OF PLANTS, John Gerard. Classic descriptions of about 2,850 plants—with over 2,700 illustrations—includes Latin and English names, physical descriptions, varieties, time and place of growth, more. 2,706 illustrations. xlv + 1,678pp. 8½ × 12¼. 23147-X Cloth. $75.00

DOROTHY AND THE WIZARD IN OZ, L. Frank Baum. Dorothy and the Wizard visit the center of the Earth, where people are vegetables, glass houses grow and Oz characters reappear. Classic sequel to *Wizard of Oz*. 256pp. 5⅜ × 8. 24714-7 Pa. $4.95

SONGS OF EXPERIENCE: Facsimile Reproduction with 26 Plates in Full Color, William Blake. This facsimile of Blake's original "Illuminated Book" reproduces 26 full-color plates from a rare 1826 edition. Includes "The Tyger," "London," "Holy Thursday," and other immortal poems. 26 color plates. Printed text of poems. 48pp. 5¼ × 7. 24636-1 Pa. $3.50

SONGS OF INNOCENCE, William Blake. The first and most popular of Blake's famous "Illuminated Books," in a facsimile edition reproducing all 31 brightly colored plates. Additional printed text of each poem. 64pp. 5¼ × 7. 22764-2 Pa. $3.50

PRECIOUS STONES, Max Bauer. Classic, thorough study of diamonds, rubies, emeralds, garnets, etc.: physical character, occurrence, properties, use, similar topics. 20 plates, 8 in color. 94 figures. 659pp. 6⅛ × 9¼. 21910-0, 21911-9 Pa., Two-vol. set $15.90

ENCYCLOPEDIA OF VICTORIAN NEEDLEWORK, S. F. A. Caulfeild and Blanche Saward. Full, precise descriptions of stitches, techniques for dozens of needlecrafts—most exhaustive reference of its kind. Over 800 figures. Total of 679pp. 8⅛ × 11. Two volumes. Vol. 1 22800-2 Pa. $11.95
Vol. 2 22801-0 Pa. $11.95

THE MARVELOUS LAND OF OZ, L. Frank Baum. Second Oz book, the Scarecrow and Tin Woodman are back with hero named Tip, Oz magic. 136 illustrations. 287pp. 5⅜ × 8½. 20692-0 Pa. $5.95

WILD FOWL DECOYS, Joel Barber. Basic book on the subject, by foremost authority and collector. Reveals history of decoy making and rigging, place in American culture, different kinds of decoys, how to make them, and how to use them. 140 plates. 156pp. 7⅞ × 10¾. 20011-6 Pa. $8.95

HISTORY OF LACE, Mrs. Bury Palliser. Definitive, profusely illustrated chronicle of lace from earliest times to late 19th century. Laces of Italy, Greece, England, France, Belgium, etc. Landmark of needlework scholarship. 266 illustrations. 672pp. 6⅛ × 9¼. 24742-2 Pa. $14.95

ILLUSTRATED GUIDE TO SHAKER FURNITURE, Robert Meader. All furniture and appurtenances, with much on unknown local styles. 235 photos. 146pp. 9 × 12. 22819-3 Pa. $7.95

WHALE SHIPS AND WHALING: A Pictorial Survey, George Francis Dow. Over 200 vintage engravings, drawings, photographs of barks, brigs, cutters, other vessels. Also harpoons, lances, whaling guns, many other artifacts. Comprehensive text by foremost authority. 207 black-and-white illustrations. 288pp. 6 × 9. 24808-9 Pa. $8.95

THE BERTRAMS, Anthony Trollope. Powerful portrayal of blind self-will and thwarted ambition includes one of Trollope's most heartrending love stories. 497pp. 5⅜ × 8½. 25119-5 Pa. $9.95

ADVENTURES WITH A HAND LENS, Richard Headstrom. Clearly written guide to observing and studying flowers and grasses, fish scales, moth and insect wings, egg cases, buds, feathers, seeds, leaf scars, moss, molds, ferns, common crystals, etc.—all with an ordinary, inexpensive magnifying glass. 209 exact line drawings aid in your discoveries. 220pp. 5⅜ × 8½. 23330-8 Pa. $4.95

RODIN ON ART AND ARTISTS, Auguste Rodin. Great sculptor's candid, wide-ranging comments on meaning of art; great artists; relation of sculpture to poetry, painting, music; philosophy of life, more. 76 superb black-and-white illustrations of Rodin's sculpture, drawings and prints. 119pp. 8⅜ × 11¼. 24487-3 Pa. $6.95

FIFTY CLASSIC FRENCH FILMS, 1912–1982: A Pictorial Record, Anthony Slide. Memorable stills from Grand Illusion, Beauty and the Beast, Hiroshima, Mon Amour, many more. Credits, plot synopses, reviews, etc. 160pp. 8¼ × 11. 25256-6 Pa. $11.95

THE PRINCIPLES OF PSYCHOLOGY, William James. Famous long course complete, unabridged. Stream of thought, time perception, memory, experimental methods; great work decades ahead of its time. 94 figures. 1,391pp. 5⅜ × 8½. 20381-6, 20382-4 Pa., Two-vol. set $23.90

BODIES IN A BOOKSHOP, R. T. Campbell. Challenging mystery of blackmail and murder with ingenious plot and superbly drawn characters. In the best tradition of British suspense fiction. 192pp. 5⅜ × 8½. 24720-1 Pa. $3.95

CALLAS: PORTRAIT OF A PRIMA DONNA, George Jellinek. Renowned commentator on the musical scene chronicles incredible career and life of the most controversial, fascinating, influential operatic personality of our time. 64 black-and-white photographs. 416pp. 5⅜ × 8¼. 25047-4 Pa. $8.95

GEOMETRY, RELATIVITY AND THE FOURTH DIMENSION, Rudolph Rucker. Exposition of fourth dimension, concepts of relativity as Flatland characters continue adventures. Popular, easily followed yet accurate, profound. 141 illustrations. 133pp. 5⅜ × 8½. 23400-2 Pa. $3.95

HOUSEHOLD STORIES BY THE BROTHERS GRIMM, with pictures by Walter Crane. 53 classic stories—Rumpelstiltskin, Rapunzel, Hansel and Gretel, the Fisherman and his Wife, Snow White, Tom Thumb, Sleeping Beauty, Cinderella, and so much more—lavishly illustrated with original 19th century drawings. 114 illustrations. x + 269pp. 5⅜ × 8½. 21080-4 Pa. $4.95

SUNDIALS, Albert Waugh. Far and away the best, most thorough coverage of ideas, mathematics concerned, types, construction, adjusting anywhere. Over 100 illustrations. 230pp. 5⅜ × 8½. 22947-5 Pa. $4.95

PICTURE HISTORY OF THE NORMANDIE: With 190 Illustrations, Frank O. Braynard. Full story of legendary French ocean liner: Art Deco interiors, design innovations, furnishings, celebrities, maiden voyage, tragic fire, much more. Extensive text. 144pp. 8⅞ × 11¾. 25257-4 Pa. $9.95

THE FIRST AMERICAN COOKBOOK: A Facsimile of "American Cookery," 1796, Amelia Simmons. Facsimile of the first American-written cookbook published in the United States contains authentic recipes for colonial favorites— pumpkin pudding, winter squash pudding, spruce beer, Indian slapjacks, and more. Introductory Essay and Glossary of colonial cooking terms. 80pp. 5⅜ × 8½. 24710-4 Pa. $3.50

101 PUZZLES IN THOUGHT AND LOGIC, C. R. Wylie, Jr. Solve murders and robberies, find out which fishermen are liars, how a blind man could possibly identify a color—purely by your own reasoning! 107pp. 5⅜ × 8½. 20367-0 Pa. $2.50

THE BOOK OF WORLD-FAMOUS MUSIC—CLASSICAL, POPULAR AND FOLK, James J. Fuld. Revised and enlarged republication of landmark work in musico-bibliography. Full information about nearly 1,000 songs and compositions including first lines of music and lyrics. New supplement. Index. 800pp. 5⅜ × 8¼. 24857-7 Pa. $14.95

ANTHROPOLOGY AND MODERN LIFE, Franz Boas. Great anthropologist's classic treatise on race and culture. Introduction by Ruth Bunzel. Only inexpensive paperback edition. 255pp. 5⅜ × 8½. 25245-0 Pa. $5.95

THE TALE OF PETER RABBIT, Beatrix Potter. The inimitable Peter's terrifying adventure in Mr. McGregor's garden, with all 27 wonderful, full-color Potter illustrations. 55pp. 4¼ × 5½. (Available in U.S. only) 22827-4 Pa. $1.75

THREE PROPHETIC SCIENCE FICTION NOVELS, H. G. Wells. *When the Sleeper Wakes, A Story of the Days to Come* and *The Time Machine* (full version). 335pp. 5⅜ × 8½. (Available in U.S. only) 20605-X Pa. $6.95

APICIUS COOKERY AND DINING IN IMPERIAL ROME, edited and translated by Joseph Dommers Vehling. Oldest known cookbook in existence offers readers a clear picture of what foods Romans ate, how they prepared them, etc. 49 illustrations. 301pp. 6⅛ × 9¼. 23563-7 Pa. $7.95

SHAKESPEARE LEXICON AND QUOTATION DICTIONARY, Alexander Schmidt. Full definitions, locations, shades of meaning of every word in plays and poems. More than 50,000 exact quotations. 1,485pp. 6½ × 9¼. 22726-X, 22727-8 Pa., Two-vol. set $29.90

THE WORLD'S GREAT SPEECHES, edited by Lewis Copeland and Lawrence W. Lamm. Vast collection of 278 speeches from Greeks to 1970. Powerful and effective models; unique look at history. 842pp. 5⅜ × 8½. 20468-5 Pa. $11.95

THE BLUE FAIRY BOOK, Andrew Lang. The first, most famous collection, with many familiar tales: Little Red Riding Hood, Aladdin and the Wonderful Lamp, Puss in Boots, Sleeping Beauty, Hansel and Gretel, Rumpelstiltskin; 37 in all. 138 illustrations. 390pp. 5⅜ × 8½. 21437-0 Pa. $6.95

THE STORY OF THE CHAMPIONS OF THE ROUND TABLE, Howard Pyle. Sir Launcelot, Sir Tristram and Sir Percival in spirited adventures of love and triumph retold in Pyle's inimitable style. 50 drawings, 31 full-page. xviii + 329pp. 6½ × 9¼. 21883-X Pa. $6.95

AUDUBON AND HIS JOURNALS, Maria Audubon. Unmatched two-volume portrait of the great artist, naturalist and author contains his journals, an excellent biography by his granddaughter, expert annotations by the noted ornithologist, Dr. Elliott Coues, and 37 superb illustrations. Total of 1,200pp. 5⅜ × 8.
Vol. I 25143-8 Pa. $8.95
Vol. II 25144-6 Pa. $8.95

GREAT DINOSAUR HUNTERS AND THEIR DISCOVERIES, Edwin H. Colbert. Fascinating, lavishly illustrated chronicle of dinosaur research, 1820's to 1960. Achievements of Cope, Marsh, Brown, Buckland, Mantell, Huxley, many others. 384pp. 5¼ × 8¼. 24701-5 Pa. $7.95

THE TASTEMAKERS, Russell Lynes. Informal, illustrated social history of American taste 1850's–1950's. First popularized categories Highbrow, Lowbrow, Middlebrow. 129 illustrations. New (1979) afterword. 384pp. 6 × 9.
23993-4 Pa. $8.95

DOUBLE CROSS PURPOSES, Ronald A. Knox. A treasure hunt in the Scottish Highlands, an old map, unidentified corpse, surprise discoveries keep reader guessing in this cleverly intricate tale of financial skullduggery. 2 black-and-white maps. 320pp. 5⅜ × 8½. (Available in U.S. only) 25032-6 Pa. $5.95

AUTHENTIC VICTORIAN DECORATION AND ORNAMENTATION IN FULL COLOR: 46 Plates from "Studies in Design," Christopher Dresser. Superb full-color lithographs reproduced from rare original portfolio of a major Victorian designer. 48pp. 9¼ × 12¼. 25083-0 Pa. $7.95

PRIMITIVE ART, Franz Boas. Remains the best text ever prepared on subject, thoroughly discussing Indian, African, Asian, Australian, and, especially, Northern American primitive art. Over 950 illustrations show ceramics, masks, totem poles, weapons, textiles, paintings, much more. 376pp. 5⅜ × 8. 20025-6 Pa. $6.95

SIDELIGHTS ON RELATIVITY, Albert Einstein. Unabridged republication of two lectures delivered by the great physicist in 1920–21. *Ether and Relativity* and *Geometry and Experience*. Elegant ideas in non-mathematical form, accessible to intelligent layman. vi + 56pp. 5⅜ × 8½. 24511-X Pa. $2.95

THE WIT AND HUMOR OF OSCAR WILDE, edited by Alvin Redman. More than 1,000 ripostes, paradoxes, wisecracks: Work is the curse of the drinking classes, I can resist everything except temptation, etc. 258pp. 5⅜ × 8½. 20602-5 Pa. $4.50

ADVENTURES WITH A MICROSCOPE, Richard Headstrom. 59 adventures with clothing fibers, protozoa, ferns and lichens, roots and leaves, much more. 142 illustrations. 232pp. 5⅜ × 8½. 23471-1 Pa. $3.95

PLANTS OF THE BIBLE, Harold N. Moldenke and Alma L. Moldenke. Standard reference to all 230 plants mentioned in Scriptures. Latin name, biblical reference, uses, modern identity, much more. Unsurpassed encyclopedic resource for scholars, botanists, nature lovers, students of Bible. Bibliography. Indexes. 123 black-and-white illustrations. 384pp. 6 × 9. 25069-5 Pa. $8.95

FAMOUS AMERICAN WOMEN: A Biographical Dictionary from Colonial Times to the Present, Robert McHenry, ed. From Pocahontas to Rosa Parks, 1,035 distinguished American women documented in separate biographical entries. Accurate, up-to-date data, numerous categories, spans 400 years. Indices. 493pp. 6½ × 9¼. 24523-3 Pa. $9.95

THE FABULOUS INTERIORS OF THE GREAT OCEAN LINERS IN HIS-TORIC PHOTOGRAPHS, William H. Miller, Jr. Some 200 superb photographs capture exquisite interiors of world's great "floating palaces"—1890's to 1980's: *Titanic, Ile de France, Queen Elizabeth, United States, Europa,* more. Approx. 200 black-and-white photographs. Captions. Text. Introduction. 160pp. 8⅜ × 11¼. 24756-2 Pa. $9.95

THE GREAT LUXURY LINERS, 1927–1954: A Photographic Record, William H. Miller, Jr. Nostalgic tribute to heyday of ocean liners. 186 photos of Ile de France, Normandie, Leviathan, Queen Elizabeth, United States, many others. Interior and exterior views. Introduction. Captions. 160pp. 9 × 12. 24056-8 Pa. $10.95

A NATURAL HISTORY OF THE DUCKS, John Charles Phillips. Great landmark of ornithology offers complete detailed coverage of nearly 200 species and subspecies of ducks: gadwall, sheldrake, merganser, pintail, many more. 74 full-color plates, 102 black-and-white. Bibliography. Total of 1,920pp. 8⅜ × 11¼. 25141-1, 25142-X Cloth. Two-vol. set $100.00

THE SEAWEED HANDBOOK: An Illustrated Guide to Seaweeds from North Carolina to Canada, Thomas F. Lee. Concise reference covers 78 species. Scientific and common names, habitat, distribution, more. Finding keys for easy identification. 224pp. 5⅜ × 8½. 25215-9 Pa. $5.95

THE TEN BOOKS OF ARCHITECTURE: The 1755 Leoni Edition, Leon Battista Alberti. Rare classic helped introduce the glories of ancient architecture to the Renaissance. 68 black-and-white plates. 336pp. 8⅜ × 11¼. 25239-6 Pa. $14.95

MISS MACKENZIE, Anthony Trollope. Minor masterpieces by Victorian master unmasks many truths about life in 19th-century England. First inexpensive edition in years. 392pp. 5⅜ × 8½. 25201-9 Pa. $7.95

THE RIME OF THE ANCIENT MARINER, Gustave Doré, Samuel Taylor Coleridge. Dramatic engravings considered by many to be his greatest work. The terrifying space of the open sea, the storms and whirlpools of an unknown ocean, the ice of Antarctica, more—all rendered in a powerful, chilling manner. Full text. 38 plates. 77pp. 9¼ × 12. 22305-1 Pa. $4.95

THE EXPEDITIONS OF ZEBULON MONTGOMERY PIKE, Zebulon Mont-gomery Pike. Fascinating first-hand accounts (1805-6) of exploration of Missis-sippi River, Indian wars, capture by Spanish dragoons, much more. 1,088pp. 5⅜ × 8½. 25254-X, 25255-8 Pa. Two-vol. set $23.90

A CONCISE HISTORY OF PHOTOGRAPHY: Third Revised Edition, Helmut Gernsheim. Best one-volume history—camera obscura, photochemistry, daguerreotypes, evolution of cameras, film, more. Also artistic aspects—landscape, portraits, fine art, etc. 281 black-and-white photographs. 26 in color. 176pp. 8⅜ × 11¼. 25128-4 Pa. $13.95

THE DORÉ BIBLE ILLUSTRATIONS, Gustave Doré. 241 detailed plates from the Bible: the Creation scenes, Adam and Eve, Flood, Babylon, battle sequences, life of Jesus, etc. Each plate is accompanied by the verses from the King James version of the Bible. 241pp. 9 × 12. 23004-X Pa. $8.95

HUGGER-MUGGER IN THE LOUVRE, Elliot Paul. Second Homer Evans mystery-comedy. Theft at the Louvre involves sleuth in hilarious, madcap caper. "A knockout."—Books. 336pp. 5⅜ × 8½. 25185-3 Pa. $5.95

FLATLAND, E. A. Abbott. Intriguing and enormously popular science-fiction classic explores the complexities of trying to survive as a two-dimensional being in a three-dimensional world. Amusingly illustrated by the author. 16 illustrations. 103pp. 5⅜ × 8½. 20001-9 Pa. $2.25

THE HISTORY OF THE LEWIS AND CLARK EXPEDITION, Meriwether Lewis and William Clark, edited by Elliott Coues. Classic edition of Lewis and Clark's day-by-day journals that later became the basis for U.S. claims to Oregon and the West. Accurate and invaluable geographical, botanical, biological, meteorological and anthropological material. Total of 1,508pp. 5⅜ × 8½.
21268-8, 21269-6, 21270-X Pa. Three-vol. set $26.85

LANGUAGE, TRUTH AND LOGIC, Alfred J. Ayer. Famous, clear introduction to Vienna, Cambridge schools of Logical Positivism. Role of philosophy, elimination of metaphysics, nature of analysis, etc. 160pp. 5⅜ × 8½. (Available in U.S. and Canada only) 20010-8 Pa. $2.95

MATHEMATICS FOR THE NONMATHEMATICIAN, Morris Kline. Detailed, college-level treatment of mathematics in cultural and historical context, with numerous exercises. For liberal arts students. Preface. Recommended Reading Lists. Tables. Index. Numerous black-and-white figures. xvi + 641pp. 5⅜ × 8½.
24823-2 Pa. $11.95

28 SCIENCE FICTION STORIES, H. G. Wells. Novels, *Star Begotten* and *Men Like Gods*, plus 26 short stories: "Empire of the Ants," "A Story of the Stone Age," "The Stolen Bacillus," "In the Abyss," etc. 915pp. 5⅜ × 8½. (Available in U.S. only)
20265-8 Cloth. $10.95

HANDBOOK OF PICTORIAL SYMBOLS, Rudolph Modley. 3,250 signs and symbols, many systems in full; official or heavy commercial use. Arranged by subject. Most in Pictorial Archive series. 143pp. 8⅛ × 11. 23357-X Pa. $6.95

INCIDENTS OF TRAVEL IN YUCATAN, John L. Stephens. Classic (1843) exploration of jungles of Yucatan, looking for evidences of Maya civilization. Travel adventures, Mexican and Indian culture, etc. Total of 669pp. 5⅜ × 8½.
20926-1, 20927-X Pa., Two-vol. set $9.90

DEGAS: An Intimate Portrait, Ambroise Vollard. Charming, anecdotal memoir by famous art dealer of one of the greatest 19th-century French painters. 14 black-and-white illustrations. Introduction by Harold L. Van Doren. 96pp. 5⅜ × 8½.
25131-4 Pa. $3.95

PERSONAL NARRATIVE OF A PILGRIMAGE TO ALMANDINAH AND MECCAH, Richard Burton. Great travel classic by remarkably colorful personality. Burton, disguised as a Moroccan, visited sacred shrines of Islam, narrowly escaping death. 47 illustrations. 959pp. 5⅜ × 8½.   21217-3, 21218-1 Pa., Two-vol. set $19.90

PHRASE AND WORD ORIGINS, A. H. Holt. Entertaining, reliable, modern study of more than 1,200 colorful words, phrases, origins and histories. Much unexpected information. 254pp. 5⅜ × 8½.   20758-7 Pa. $5.95

THE RED THUMB MARK, R. Austin Freeman. In this first Dr. Thorndyke case, the great scientific detective draws fascinating conclusions from the nature of a single fingerprint. Exciting story, authentic science. 320pp. 5⅜ × 8½. (Available in U.S. only)   25210-8 Pa. $5.95

AN EGYPTIAN HIEROGLYPHIC DICTIONARY, E. A. Wallis Budge. Monumental work containing about 25,000 words or terms that occur in texts ranging from 3000 B.C. to 600 A.D. Each entry consists of a transliteration of the word, the word in hieroglyphs, and the meaning in English. 1,314pp. 6⅜ × 10.
23615-3, 23616-1 Pa., Two-vol. set $31.90

THE COMPLEAT STRATEGYST: Being a Primer on the Theory of Games of Strategy, J. D. Williams. Highly entertaining classic describes, with many illustrated examples, how to select best strategies in conflict situations. Prefaces. Appendices. xvi + 268pp. 5⅜ × 8½.   25101-2 Pa. $5.95

THE ROAD TO OZ, L. Frank Baum. Dorothy meets the Shaggy Man, little Button-Bright and the Rainbow's beautiful daughter in this delightful trip to the magical Land of Oz. 272pp. 5⅜ × 8.   25208-6 Pa. $4.95

POINT AND LINE TO PLANE, Wassily Kandinsky. Seminal exposition of role of point, line, other elements in non-objective painting. Essential to understanding 20th-century art. 127 illustrations. 192pp. 6½ × 9¼.   23808-3 Pa. $4.95

LADY ANNA, Anthony Trollope. Moving chronicle of Countess Lovel's bitter struggle to win for herself and daughter Anna their rightful rank and fortune—perhaps at cost of sanity itself. 384pp. 5⅜ × 8½.   24669-8 Pa. $8.95

EGYPTIAN MAGIC, E. A. Wallis Budge. Sums up all that is known about magic in Ancient Egypt: the role of magic in controlling the gods, powerful amulets that warded off evil spirits, scarabs of immortality, use of wax images, formulas and spells, the secret name, much more. 253pp. 5⅜ × 8½.   22681-6 Pa. $4.50

THE DANCE OF SIVA, Ananda Coomaraswamy. Preeminent authority unfolds the vast metaphysic of India: the revelation of her art, conception of the universe, social organization, etc. 27 reproductions of art masterpieces. 192pp. 5⅜ × 8½.
24817-8 Pa. $5.95

CHRISTMAS CUSTOMS AND TRADITIONS, Clement A. Miles. Origin, evolution, significance of religious, secular practices. Caroling, gifts, yule logs, much more. Full, scholarly yet fascinating; non-sectarian. 400pp. 5⅜ × 8½.
23354-5 Pa. $6.50

THE HUMAN FIGURE IN MOTION, Eadweard Muybridge. More than 4,500 stopped-action photos, in action series, showing undraped men, women, children jumping, lying down, throwing, sitting, wrestling, carrying, etc. 390pp. 7⅞ × 10⅝.
20204-6 Cloth. $21.95

THE MAN WHO WAS THURSDAY, Gilbert Keith Chesterton. Witty, fast-paced novel about a club of anarchists in turn-of-the-century London. Brilliant social, religious, philosophical speculations. 128pp. 5⅜ × 8½.　　　25121-7 Pa. $3.95

A CEZANNE SKETCHBOOK: Figures, Portraits, Landscapes and Still Lifes, Paul Cezanne. Great artist experiments with tonal effects, light, mass, other qualities in over 100 drawings. A revealing view of developing master painter, precursor of Cubism. 102 black-and-white illustrations. 144pp. 8¾ × 6⅜.　　　24790-2 Pa. $5.95

AN ENCYCLOPEDIA OF BATTLES: Accounts of Over 1,560 Battles from 1479 B.C. to the Present, David Eggenberger. Presents essential details of every major battle in recorded history, from the first battle of Megiddo in 1479 B.C. to Grenada in 1984. List of Battle Maps. New Appendix covering the years 1967–1984. Index. 99 illustrations. 544pp. 6½ × 9¼.　　　24913-1 Pa. $14.95

AN ETYMOLOGICAL DICTIONARY OF MODERN ENGLISH, Ernest Weekley. Richest, fullest work, by foremost British lexicographer. Detailed word histories. Inexhaustible. Total of 856pp. 6½ × 9¼.
21873-2, 21874-0 Pa., Two-vol. set $17.00

WEBSTER'S AMERICAN MILITARY BIOGRAPHIES, edited by Robert McHenry. Over 1,000 figures who shaped 3 centuries of American military history. Detailed biographies of Nathan Hale, Douglas MacArthur, Mary Hallaren, others. Chronologies of engagements, more. Introduction. Addenda. 1,033 entries in alphabetical order. xi + 548pp. 6½ × 9¼. (Available in U.S. only)
24758-9 Pa. $11.95

LIFE IN ANCIENT EGYPT, Adolf Erman. Detailed older account, with much not in more recent books: domestic life, religion, magic, medicine, commerce, and whatever else needed for complete picture. Many illustrations. 597pp. 5⅜ × 8½.
22632-8 Pa. $8.95

HISTORIC COSTUME IN PICTURES, Braun & Schneider. Over 1,450 costumed figures shown, covering a wide variety of peoples: kings, emperors, nobles, priests, servants, soldiers, scholars, townsfolk, peasants, merchants, courtiers, cavaliers, and more. 256pp. 8⅜ × 11¼.　　　23150-X Pa. $8.95

THE NOTEBOOKS OF LEONARDO DA VINCI, edited by J. P. Richter. Extracts from manuscripts reveal great genius; on painting, sculpture, anatomy, sciences, geography, etc. Both Italian and English. 186 ms. pages reproduced, plus 500 additional drawings, including studies for *Last Supper, Sforza* monument, etc. 860pp. 7⅞ × 10⅝. (Available in U.S. only) 22572-0, 22573-9 Pa., Two-vol. set $29.90

THE ART NOUVEAU STYLE BOOK OF ALPHONSE MUCHA: All 72 Plates from "Documents Decoratifs" in Original Color, Alphonse Mucha. Rare copyright-free design portfolio by high priest of Art Nouveau. Jewelry, wallpaper, stained glass, furniture, figure studies, plant and animal motifs, etc. Only complete one-volume edition. 80pp. 9⅜ × 12¼.   24044-4 Pa. $8.95

ANIMALS: 1,419 COPYRIGHT-FREE ILLUSTRATIONS OF MAMMALS, BIRDS, FISH, INSECTS, ETC., edited by Jim Harter. Clear wood engravings present, in extremely lifelike poses, over 1,000 species of animals. One of the most extensive pictorial sourcebooks of its kind. Captions. Index. 284pp. 9 × 12.
                                                                                23766-4 Pa. $9.95

OBELISTS FLY HIGH, C. Daly King. Masterpiece of American detective fiction, long out of print, involves murder on a 1935 transcontinental flight—"a very thrilling story"—NY Times. Unabridged and unaltered republication of the edition published by William Collins Sons & Co. Ltd., London, 1935. 288pp. 5⅜ × 8½. (Available in U.S. only)   25036-9 Pa. $4.95

VICTORIAN AND EDWARDIAN FASHION: A Photographic Survey, Alison Gernsheim. First fashion history completely illustrated by contemporary photographs. Full text plus 235 photos, 1840–1914, in which many celebrities appear. 240pp. 6½ × 9¼.   24205-6 Pa. $6.95

THE ART OF THE FRENCH ILLUSTRATED BOOK, 1700–1914, Gordon N. Ray. Over 630 superb book illustrations by Fragonard, Delacroix, Daumier, Doré, Grandville, Manet, Mucha, Steinlen, Toulouse-Lautrec and many others. Preface. Introduction. 633 halftones. Indices of artists, authors & titles, binders and provenances. Appendices. Bibliography. 608pp. 8⅜ × 11¼.   25086-5 Pa. $24.95

THE WONDERFUL WIZARD OF OZ, L. Frank Baum. Facsimile in full color of America's finest children's classic. 143 illustrations by W. W. Denslow. 267pp. 5⅜ × 8½.   20691-2 Pa. $5.95

FRONTIERS OF MODERN PHYSICS: New Perspectives on Cosmology, Relativity, Black Holes and Extraterrestrial Intelligence, Tony Rothman, et al. For the intelligent layman. Subjects include: cosmological models of the universe; black holes; the neutrino; the search for extraterrestrial intelligence. Introduction. 46 black-and-white illustrations. 192pp. 5⅜ × 8½.   24587-X Pa. $6.95

THE FRIENDLY STARS, Martha Evans Martin & Donald Howard Menzel. Classic text marshalls the stars together in an engaging, non-technical survey, presenting them as sources of beauty in night sky. 23 illustrations. Foreword. 2 star charts. Index. 147pp. 5⅜ × 8½.   21099-5 Pa. $3.50

FADS AND FALLACIES IN THE NAME OF SCIENCE, Martin Gardner. Fair, witty appraisal of cranks, quacks, and quackeries of science and pseudoscience: hollow earth, Velikovsky, orgone energy, Dianetics, flying saucers, Bridey Murphy, food and medical fads, etc. Revised, expanded In the Name of Science. "A very able and even-tempered presentation."—The New Yorker. 363pp. 5⅜ × 8.
                                                                                20394-8 Pa. $6.50

ANCIENT EGYPT: ITS CULTURE AND HISTORY, J. E Manchip White. From pre-dynastics through Ptolemies: society, history, political structure, religion, daily life, literature, cultural heritage. 48 plates. 217pp. 5⅜ × 8½.   22548-8 Pa. $5.95

SIR HARRY HOTSPUR OF HUMBLETHWAITE, Anthony Trollope. Incisive, unconventional psychological study of a conflict between a wealthy baronet, his idealistic daughter, and their scapegrace cousin. The 1870 novel in its first inexpensive edition in years. 250pp. 5⅜ × 8½. 24953-0 Pa. $5.95

LASERS AND HOLOGRAPHY, Winston E. Kock. Sound introduction to burgeoning field, expanded (1981) for second edition. Wave patterns, coherence, lasers, diffraction, zone plates, properties of holograms, recent advances. 84 illustrations. 160pp. 5⅜ × 8¼. (Except in United Kingdom) 24041-X Pa. $3.50

INTRODUCTION TO ARTIFICIAL INTELLIGENCE: SECOND, EN-LARGED EDITION, Philip C. Jackson, Jr. Comprehensive survey of artificial intelligence—the study of how machines (computers) can be made to act intelligently. Includes introductory and advanced material. Extensive notes updating the main text. 132 black-and-white illustrations. 512pp. 5⅜ × 8½. 24864-X Pa. $8.95

HISTORY OF INDIAN AND INDONESIAN ART, Ananda K. Coomaraswamy. Over 400 illustrations illuminate classic study of Indian art from earliest Harappa finds to early 20th century. Provides philosophical, religious and social insights. 304pp. 6⅜ × 9⅜. 25005-9 Pa. $8.95

THE GOLEM, Gustav Meyrink. Most famous supernatural novel in modern European literature, set in Ghetto of Old Prague around 1890. Compelling story of mystical experiences, strange transformations, profound terror. 13 black-and-white illustrations. 224pp. 5⅜ × 8½. (Available in U.S. only) 25025-3 Pa. $6.95

ARMADALE, Wilkie Collins. Third great mystery novel by the author of *The Woman in White* and *The Moonstone*. Original magazine version with 40 illustrations. 597pp. 5⅜ × 8½. 23429-0 Pa. $9.95

PICTORIAL ENCYCLOPEDIA OF HISTORIC ARCHITECTURAL PLANS, DETAILS AND ELEMENTS: With 1,880 Line Drawings of Arches, Domes, Doorways, Facades, Gables, Windows, etc., John Theodore Haneman. Sourcebook of inspiration for architects, designers, others. Bibliography. Captions. 141pp. 9 × 12. 24605-1 Pa. $6.95

BENCHLEY LOST AND FOUND, Robert Benchley. Finest humor from early 30's, about pet peeves, child psychologists, post office and others. Mostly unavailable elsewhere. 73 illustrations by Peter Arno and others. 183pp. 5⅜ × 8½. 22410-4 Pa. $3.95

ERTÉ GRAPHICS, Erté. Collection of striking color graphics: *Seasons, Alphabet, Numerals, Aces* and *Precious Stones*. 50 plates, including 4 on covers. 48pp. 9⅜ × 12¼. 23580-7 Pa. $6.95

THE JOURNAL OF HENRY D. THOREAU, edited by Bradford Torrey, F. H. Allen. Complete reprinting of 14 volumes, 1837–61, over two million words; the sourcebooks for *Walden*, etc. Definitive. All original sketches, plus 75 photographs. 1,804pp. 8½ × 12¼. 20312-3, 20313-1 Cloth., Two-vol. set $80.00

CASTLES: THEIR CONSTRUCTION AND HISTORY, Sidney Toy. Traces castle development from ancient roots. Nearly 200 photographs and drawings illustrate moats, keeps, baileys, many other features. Caernarvon, Dover Castles, Hadrian's Wall, Tower of London, dozens more. 256pp. 5⅜ × 8¼. 24898-4 Pa. $5.95

AMERICAN CLIPPER SHIPS: 1833–1858, Octavius T. Howe & Frederick C. Matthews. Fully-illustrated, encyclopedic review of 352 clipper ships from the period of America's greatest maritime supremacy. Introduction. 109 halftones. 5 black-and-white line illustrations. Index. Total of 928pp. 5⅜ × 8½.
25115-2, 25116-0 Pa., Two-vol. set $17.90

TOWARDS A NEW ARCHITECTURE, Le Corbusier. Pioneering manifesto by great architect, near legendary founder of "International School." Technical and aesthetic theories, views on industry, economics, relation of form to function, "mass-production spirit," much more. Profusely illustrated. Unabridged translation of 13th French edition. Introduction by Frederick Etchells. 320pp. 6⅛ × 9¼. (Available in U.S. only)
25023-7 Pa. $8.95

THE BOOK OF KELLS, edited by Blanche Cirker. Inexpensive collection of 32 full-color, full-page plates from the greatest illuminated manuscript of the Middle Ages, painstakingly reproduced from rare facsimile edition. Publisher's Note. Captions. 32pp. 9⅜ × 12¼.
24345-1 Pa. $4.95

BEST SCIENCE FICTION STORIES OF H. G. WELLS, H. G. Wells. Full novel *The Invisible Man*, plus 17 short stories: "The Crystal Egg," "Aepyornis Island," "The Strange Orchid," etc. 303pp. 5⅜ × 8½. (Available in U.S. only)
21531-8 Pa. $6.95

AMERICAN SAILING SHIPS: Their Plans and History, Charles G. Davis. Photos, construction details of schooners, frigates, clippers, other sailcraft of 18th to early 20th centuries—plus entertaining discourse on design, rigging, nautical lore, much more. 137 black-and-white illustrations. 240pp. 6⅛ × 9¼.
24658-2 Pa. $6.95

ENTERTAINING MATHEMATICAL PUZZLES, Martin Gardner. Selection of author's favorite conundrums involving arithmetic, money, speed, etc., with lively commentary. Complete solutions. 112pp. 5⅜ × 8½.   25211-6 Pa. $2.95

THE WILL TO BELIEVE, HUMAN IMMORTALITY, William James. Two books bound together. Effect of irrational on logical, and arguments for human immortality. 402pp. 5⅜ × 8½.   20291-7 Pa. $7.50

THE HAUNTED MONASTERY and THE CHINESE MAZE MURDERS, Robert Van Gulik. 2 full novels by Van Gulik continue adventures of Judge Dee and his companions. An evil Taoist monastery, seemingly supernatural events; overgrown topiary maze that hides strange crimes. Set in 7th-century China. 27 illustrations. 328pp. 5⅜ × 8½.   23502-5 Pa. $5.95

CELEBRATED CASES OF JUDGE DEE (DEE GOONG AN), translated by Robert Van Gulik. Authentic 18th-century Chinese detective novel; Dee and associates solve three interlocked cases. Led to Van Gulik's own stories with same characters. Extensive introduction. 9 illustrations. 237pp. 5⅜ × 8½.
23337-5 Pa. $4.95

Prices subject to change without notice.
Available at your book dealer or write for free catalog to Dept. GI, Dover Publications, Inc., 31 East 2nd St., Mineola, N.Y. 11501. Dover publishes more than 175 books each year on science, elementary and advanced mathematics, biology, music, art, literary history, social sciences and other areas.